UNBREAKABLE

Also by Ronnie O'Sullivan

Ronnie
Running

UNBREAKABLE

Ronnie O'Sullivan
with Tom Fordyce

SEVEN DIALS

First published in Great Britain in 2023 by Seven Dials
An imprint of The Orion Publishing Group Ltd
Carmelite House, 50 Victoria Embankment
London EC4Y 0DZ

An Hachette Livre Company

1 3 5 7 9 10 8 6 4 2

A CIP catalogue record for this book
is available from the British Library.

ISBN HB 9781399610018
ISBN TPB 9781399610025
ISBN eBook 9781399610049
ISBN Audio 9781399610056

Typeset by Input Data Services Ltd, Bridgwater, Somerset

Printed in Great Britain by Clays Ltd, Elcograf S.p.A.

MIX
Paper from
responsible sources
FSC® C104740

www.orionbooks.co.uk

I'd like to dedicate this book to my partner Laila;
to those who have helped me so much with my snooker,
including the late Frank Adamson, Steve Peters, Steve Feeney
and Ray Reardon; and to those who have helped so much with
my running, including Eamonn Christie, Eamonn Martin,
Shane Healy, Vince Wilson, Woodford Green Athletic Club and
Ilford Running Club.

ACKNOWLEDGEMENTS

Thank you as ever to Jonny Geller, Viola Hayden, Louise Cooke and the gang at Curtis Brown.

To the team at Orion: Vicky Eribo, Francesca Pearce, Lizzie Dorney-Kingdom, Tom Noble, Steve Marking, Natalie Dawkins, Lucinda McNeile, Tierney Witty, Nicola Thatcher and Anne O'Brien, plus David Luxton at DLA. Thank you for all your hard work on the book.

And to my writer Tom Fordyce. Tom and I had a great time putting this book together, and the process of getting from our chats to the finished article has been mind-blowing. I hope this book will help people find what works for them in life. Thank you, Tom, for putting all we spoke about into a great book.

CONTENTS

PROLOGUE

This is what it feels like when you're playing well. When you're doing, not thinking. When the snooker gods are smiling on you, not pulling you apart.

It's an energy. In your body, walking round the table. In your mind, looking at the spread of the balls, settling down behind the white, the butt of the cue sitting in your right hand, your bridge hand out on the green cloth ahead of you, middle finger pointing the way like a needle on a compass.

It's the best drug you've ever experienced. You've felt it before, but it left you, and now it's returned you recognise the lovely rush and you want it to stay forever.

A sense of total control. Doesn't matter where the balls are on the table. Maybe there's four reds all messy round the pink, a couple more on one of the cushions, not much available after this red and this black.

You don't care. Everything you're looking at makes sense. The angles you need to find, the spin and power you want to put through the cue ball. The compression.

When you're flying, the sounds all around you come in harmony.

The cue ball hits with a noise so crisp and clean you could have your eyes shut and still know the pot's going in. A thick sound – solid, not thin and brittle, like a coin dropped on a tiled floor. The ball disappears into the pocket like the echo of a drum beat: not rattling and vibrating, just in, gone. The punters in the seats around you are all soft background one moment, coos and mmms, and then roars and these sudden explosions of applause when you pull off a shot some of them never saw coming and most didn't dare to believe would come off.

They aren't dabblers, these ones up close. They've not found you by flicking through the TV channels, they're not sleeping off a big lunch on the sofa.

They're here because they love it. Most of them have tried to play snooker at some point, and they understand you're making a difficult game look ridiculously easy, and the appreciation is there for you to absorb and relish like a patch of warm sunlight on a cold morning.

There's no conscious thought about it, not some mad maths sum going on in your head about degrees and speed and impact angles.

Just you and that white, a certainty about where you need to put it, a knowledge it'll go exactly where you want. The right line, giving you options, narrowing the odds on the next shot, keeping the pot straightforward so the next one can be straightforward too.

Oh, it's beautiful when it works! You struggle and you battle, and you doubt yourself, and the ones who run the game come after you for fines and hearings and all manner of stuff you don't want to do. You don't sleep too good at night, and you're knackered all day and curling up on sofas and waking up not quite remembering where you are.

And it's all come right, in this moment, and there are things in your head that might sound flashy but are real and true.

There is no one on this planet right now who can compete with me.

That's the thought that comes in. Eight billion people in the world, and not one of them out there who can knock me off my perch. Good players at this tournament, maybe one of them sitting watching you from that chair over there, but none of them you're worried about. Not today.

You think: no one can take this game away from me.

It's all there, if I want it.

1

BEGINNINGS
HELLO, MY NAME IS RONNIE

Okay. Here's me, first thing in the morning, looking in the mirror.

I'm not one for it, instinctively. Staring at myself, thinking about what's reflecting back. Makes me feel a bit awkward. Makes me start thinking too much.

But I'm doing it now, and here's what I see. Dark green eyes. Big nose, could sort that out. Loads of hair in places where it shouldn't be – in my earholes, up my nose. The mono eyebrow, one of the reasons they used to call me Liam Gallagher's missing brother.

I think, I wish I didn't have so much hair everywhere, and then, nah, I've aged alright. There's only a little bit of grey in the sideburns, no gaps in the barnet. I think, I'm not looking too bad for forty-seven years old. Not the years I've lived through.

I was the boy wonder, once. The kid from north-east London who hung around smoky snooker halls and won money off grown men. Rosy-cheeked and innocent but a mouth like a sewer. The one they all said was going to change the world, who played on impulse and flair and pure love.

Then I was the lost boy. Out for three nights and three days at a time, piling into the Guinness and spliffs, burning all that talent up. A son whose dad was sent away to prison and whose mum went away too.

Flashy, on the outside, all fast cars and big chat. Broken, on the inside. Saved by rehab and running.

It took me a long time to become me. To become a winner – not just of matches where I could run away with it, but when I had to figure it all out. Not just the occasional tournament, but seven World Championships. To keep winning at an age when my heroes were long gone.

To become someone I could look at in the mirror and not turn away from.

Let me tell you something about snooker, from the inside. It's beautiful, and it's brutal.

I love this sport. I feel blessed to have played it to the highest level. It's in my head all day long, and I obsess about it, love its history. I'll talk to you all night about Joe Davis and Steve Davis and Stephen Hendry.

But it can be bad for that head of mine, this thing I can't let go. It can be capricious and cruel.

You and the table, all day long, every day. Low roofs and artificial lights, stale air and bad food.

All those hours in a dark room, and you not talking to anyone but yourself. Shutting down your emotions, losing your people skills, if you had the chance to develop any as an outlier kid in the first place. Participating only in one little strange corner of life.

If you play a Grand Slam final in tennis and put a forehand in the net, your chance to put it right comes along with the next rally a few moments later. You're a golfer missing a putt in one of the majors, and you'll probably have another 70-odd shots to get your round back on track. You're also the only one who can touch your ball. No other player can stick you behind a tree or clatter you into a bunker, just to make you suffer.

Snooker? It's all about ruining your opponent's life.

It's breaking their game into pieces. It's doing all the things that make them get angry and frustrated. It's fucking them up.

You can do it to yourself. Cruising through a match, playing lovely, then make one mistake, and suddenly you're powerless. Doesn't matter what other magic you've worked to that point, how much practice you've put in.

You, stuck in your chair, watching your opponent at the table. Them taking the frame away from you, potting balls, ruining your day.

Absolutely nothing you can do about it. Sit there, sip on your water, stare at the tip of your cue or into the darkness beyond the bright TV lights and the silent faces.

Of course, you try not to think about your error, about the damage it's done to your hopes. But all your brain wants to focus on is exactly that. Why it happened, what you should have done instead. Eating away at your guts, harsh and acidic inside you.

When you're at the top in sport for long enough, you figure out after a while the role the spectators want you to play. It's the Roman days and we're the gladiators. That's all you are. Out in the arena, on your own, fighting for your life.

If you win, and they carry you off on your shield, you might get all the rewards the gladiators used to get. I've hung around with Hendry and seen people look at him like they've seen a god. A man almost twenty-five years on from his last world title, and they walk up to him and in their eyes he's still at his peak, still the greatest.

Other times I see the old, faded stars who no one's looking

after anymore. The ones left filling out betting slips and going down the pub to cadge drinks off strangers.

The fans watching in the stands, on TV? They're the voyeurs. They get a great kick out of watching the two of you struggling and hurting, falling apart and trying to get up again.

There's nothing wrong with that. I do it as well. You just have to understand how it is. It's going to be hard, and it's going to be tough, so you have to be tough. You've got to find a way of coping with it all, a way of discovering a resilience you don't think you were born with.

You learn things, in this game, and that's some of the stuff I want to talk about, along with the big wins and bad defeats. The ways I've coped with the hard times and the dark times, with the pressure and the clamour and the doubts; the ways you can carry some of these ideas and techniques into your own life. Because the things that have helped me in snooker have also helped me away from the table, and maybe they can help you navigate your way through the hard times too. Working out the angles in the real world, finding your trick shots for life.

I've had to learn, because I've struggled.

There was this sensation I used to have when I was about twelve years old. Everything was flowing, and I felt . . . *superhuman*.

It was all instinctive, everything I did. I'd never had lessons. I just saw it, felt it, played it.

Can you imagine how good that feels? I could do the conjuring trick the others couldn't. I could make people go weak at the knees, and I didn't even have to think about it. It just happened.

No wonder you get obsessed. It's your secret weapon, it's your escape from everything else. Your panic room. Nothing else in the world can touch you in the same way.

Now? My relationship with sport is more complicated than when I was younger. The feeling of being superhuman is a fleeting one, often just out of reach.

It was all so uncomplicated, back then. Nothing else mattered. Just me, and the balls, and the table.

But you can't sustain that sort of devotion and guilelessness when you're no longer a kid. Other things come into your world. People let you down and use you up. It can't ever be as simple, so you need something else: foundations they can't shake; solutions, when the magic slips away and you feel nothing where before you could do the impossible.

Because it is always a battle, for me. A few months after I won the Worlds in 2022, I'd been back on the practice table for five or six days, and I felt like I couldn't pot a ball. Seven world titles behind me, and in all that week, I had maybe thirty minutes where I thought, yep, I'm flying here. As quickly as the good feeling had come in, it left me again.

Madness, isn't it? This can be your daily reality, even after thirty years of success: holed up in some chain hotel room on an industrial estate in the middle of nowhere, only there because a tournament's on at the conference centre round the corner, and the same old horrible doubts coming knocking again.

This slump is going to go on forever. This time I am never going to come out of it.

That's the great fear that haunts me. I'll talk to my mentor Steve Peters, and it'll all come tumbling out. Steve, I'm too old, I'm too frazzled. Hendry was done years before me, Davis was playing for fun rather than trophies by the time he was thirty. Steve, I'm scared the wheels have come off. I don't want to be that deluded sportsman who carries on ten years longer than he should have done. Life's too short to suffer like this.

And he'll go, 'Ron, you've been saying this for the last ten years. Ten years when you've won four world titles. Look back at your career like the rest of the world does: all those World Championships, but seven Masters titles too, and seven UK Championships. No one else in history has won that many Triple Crown titles. World number one, again and again. More ranking titles than anyone else ever, more century breaks, more maximums. The fastest ever 147.

'Ron, I'll tell you when the wheels are coming off. If you're making quarter-finals, semi-finals for eighteen months and you're not making finals, the wheels have come off. Until then, just go out and play and enjoy it.'

He's right. The snooker gods always reward you. You might go out early in your first couple of tournaments, then reach a quarter, then a semi. There might be a couple of finals, and you don't win them. Then, just before the World Championships, the superpower returns.

You win the Worlds, with that energy, with it all making sense – the angles you need to find, the side, the compression – and you go, wow, how the hell did that happen?

Hello, my name is Ronnie. I'm a snooker player, and a recovering addict.

I was addicted to alcohol, to drugs. I didn't know myself as a man until rehab. I only knew what other people wanted me to be.

I'll tell you it all, here and now. I'll tell you how I won those world titles, how I hope to win more. Thirty years of being a professional snooker player, a few more to come, no matter how much grey appears in those sideburns.

You can come and have a stroll round my head, if you want. I'll tell you how I've made it through. There's good stuff and bad stuff, things I'm proud about and things I got wrong. A lot of things I got wrong.

I haven't got all the answers. I'm not the sort who fancies himself. But I'm always chasing them, and if you've messed up as often as I have, you learn stuff along the way. You listen to other people who know more than you, who have spent lifetimes trying to figure out how we can all steer a path through the problems we'll face. I've been lucky with the people I've met, and I've borrowed plenty from them, and I've learned from my own experiences too: the wild days, the rehab; the doubts and crises; the world titles, and the pleasures and pressures they bring.

Because it fascinates me, this stuff. The simple things we can all do, the micro-adjustments that can make such a big difference. But I'm not perfect. Sometimes I'm all over the place. I'm a reactor; I get punched in the head and then I respond.

If you want something in your life that gives you joy, whether it's snooker, or a relationship, or a cause, you have to accept the good with the bad. Anyway, perfection is dangerous, because perfection doesn't exist. I don't believe in it – not for how you live your life, not for how you try to play snooker.

People come up to you after a match, when you're playing well, and they shake their heads and smile in that funny way like they've just seen some cool magic trick and they can't work out how it's done. They look at you and say, 'Ronnie, you're like a panther out there!' Smooth and easy, prowling, eyes on your prey.

That's where you want to be, all the time. Me controlling the snooker, not the snooker controlling me. Feeding off the crowd, the atmosphere.

When you get to that place, it's like nothing else in your life. For once, it all seems to make sense.

I belong.

That's what you think.

Here's something that's taken me almost all my life to appreciate: being one of the best ever at what you do is immensely satisfying. It's there when you go to bed at night, like a cosy blanket, and it's there when you wake in the morning, like the comfort of your first cup of tea.

When I'm hitting the white ball solid and strong – and my game is all about cue ball control – it makes me feel less insecure as a person. I know it's crazy, but that's the way it is. And then it slips away, and you chase it and chase it and consider anything to get it back. I've had imposter syndrome. I used to think that everyone else was collaborating to let me win – players, referees, organisers – because I'd win tournaments and I'd think I'd played so poorly that there's no way in a million years it could have been possible any other way.

There's times when I've won and I've wanted to give everyone in the room their money back. Times I've won and still felt like a loser.

You ignore the scoreboard that says you won easy, and you go back to the dressing room with your cue in your right hand. You undo your waistcoat and kick off the smart shoes and sit there with your cup of tea and think, *mate, I was rubbish out there.*

Then you watch it back on telly, lying on the bed in your hotel room, and it's like looking at a different man. He's playing lovely snooker. He's a million times better than you thought.

You've doubted yourself, so you think this geezer who looks like you but can't be you must be bluffing it. Styling it out. But it's so natural, the way he's moving round the table. You can see the bounce in the step, the rhythm from shot to shot. Standing square behind the ball. Chalk from right pocket onto cue tip, two downstrokes, tucking it away again. Settling into his stance without a doubt in his mind.

Massive highs, massive lows. That was always how it was for me. It's no way to live your life, out on those emotional extremes.

I'm playing well, I'm buzzing. Right, we're all going out tonight, we're going here, there and everywhere. Drinks on me, who's coming?

I'm playing badly. No bounce in my step, no gliding round the table. Feeling heavy, now. I'm not a panther, I'm a bear. Lumpy, grumpy. Hairy and ugly.

I used to shut myself away in the house. Didn't want to know, didn't want to see anyone. Didn't face the world.

So many knocks, so little time and space to recover. Snooker is not a sport where you get to pick and choose who you play and when you play them. You've got to take on all comers, week after week, town after town. It's the most punishing sort of meritocracy; the deeper you go into a tournament, the harder the battle ahead.

If you're a boxer, you can have your career managed. Avoid that dangerous puncher, swerve this one until he's older, fill out your record and wallet with some easy ones. Some stooges.

Snooker doesn't give you that luxury. It's a sport that requires repetition. Repetition requires hours. You're not going to get away with an hour and a half training like many Premier League footballers do. You've got to put your four or five hours a day in, most days, even the top few guys. For the players just outside the top ten, floating around looking for ranking points and shots at semi-finals and further, you have to work harder still. Six hours a day, seven hours a day.

Forget the trophies for a moment. I have been the undisputed world champion of self-sabotage. I could take something beautiful and fret at it and squeeze it until all the pleasure and life had gone.

I didn't understand what was happening. As it got worse, I'd panic more, accelerate the death-spiral. And it had nowhere to go.

You think snooker is a calm sport. We wear smart shoes and bow ties. We show almost no public emotion. We don't shout and we don't scream, and we have no team-mates to jump into their arms.

So it all stays in your head, when you're falling apart. Like we're Victorian statesmen rather than fragile young men. The outward appearance of mannequins in a tailor's window, when inside we feel like rock stars who've lost the ability to write a killer riff.

Something else from the inside of elite sport. Most of the time you're a loser. Even when I'm number one in the world and reigning world champion, I lose more tournaments than I win.

Maybe it's making sense now. What it does to your head, all this stuff that looks so easy and enjoyable from the outside. How a sport is only a sport but ends up defining everything in your life. How something that brings you more pleasure and satisfaction than anything else can also be your great torment and mortal enemy.

Why do we do it? For the sense of peace, when the magic comes. The sense of control.

There is no one on this planet right now who can compete with me.

When you're outplaying another great player in a critical frame, it's like having a fish on a hook. Twitching, struggling, fighting for air. Forcing them into mistakes – not big ones, because this is the elite, the best in the world – but small incremental increases of pressure, every shot making it that tiny bit harder for them to get the cue ball where they want it.

It doesn't always have to be a great pot or a big break. It might simply be the way you're hitting the ball. That thick, solid noise. We all recognise it. Your opponent hears you striking the ball sweet and it puts doubt in his mind.

This geezer's on it today. I'm in trouble. I'll have to take risks.

There's another motivation I've stumbled upon in this last decade: the satisfaction that comes from working your way through those crises.

I used to think talent was the only way to win. I thought if you slogged your way through you were a fraud. It was pure ability or nothing.

Graft was for the players who couldn't feel like I could feel. Grafting was easy. It was cheaper than skill. I was always led by my wayward mind, wherever it wanted to go. Mind feels good, yep, we're in business. Mind feels bad, I'm out of here.

Now, coming up towards my own personal half-century, I've learned to take comfort from the graft. I love working on little nuances of the game on the table. I love tinkering, because you never quite know what's going to come from it. I love working out the answer.

This book is about survival. It's about love and obsession and failure, as much as winning. It's about offering yourself up to the snooker gods and seeing what they choose to throw back at you.

And it's about choice: the way you live your life, the people you let inside. The temptations and the mistakes, the discipline and the dedication. The ways we can make things better for ourselves.

When I talk about being unbreakable. I don't mean that I never crack. I don't mean I never struggle.

It's about navigating your way through the bad days and the good days. It's finding ways to get off your knees and keep going. That's what unbreakable is to me: finding things easy sometimes, and almost impossible at other times, but never letting it destroy you. Because when the call to the arena comes, I choose to be a gladiator. Forty-seven years old, and I'm still fighting, when I should have been wrecked at twenty-five, when I was on the rocks and couldn't get off.

I've been in that place where all my happiness was wrapped up in how I played snooker. I was chasing it, and the more I chased it, the more it wasn't there.

I can't chase it anymore. I don't want that life, I don't want to be that person. I want to be present in whatever I am doing, not lost in myself. To look at myself in the mirror, and smile.

This is the story of how the golden kid and the lost boy escaped their fate. How a man grew up to find a better way forward.

To put himself back together. To become unbreakable.

2

WORLDS PART I
GRAB IT BY THE BALLS

I'm in my dressing room at the Crucible. Monday night, the May Day bank holiday. The final session of the World Championship final, the last session of my season.

It's grey in here and it's sterile. Concrete breeze blocks with a thin layer of paint. In the early rounds you notice it, but not now. We've been here seventeen days. It feels like home.

It feels like exactly where I want to be. So many tournaments where the voice in my head is telling me I don't want to be there, that I'd rather be at home with no one bothering me, going for my run early in the morning in Hainault Forest, taking my Bichon Maltese, Osho, for his walks. Making dinner with Laila, keeping my head clean and straight.

Not here. Not at the Crucible. All I want to do when I get to Sheffield is stay here for as long as I can.

It's the quarter-finals when you start getting excited. That's when you feel you can make this final. When you know you have a chance of winning it. You're into the rhythm of it then. Your game is settled.

There's a couple of small dressing rooms here, a couple of larger ones. They move you around in the early rounds; first round you could be in 1, second round you could be in 3. Now there's only me and my opponent left in of the thirty-two of us who turned up two and a half weeks ago, we're in the larger ones, and I'm making it my space. Clearing all the clutter they leave in there for you, the coffee cups and biscuits and waters. Me and my mate Robbie, making room for what I need – my cue case, my phone, my shopping bag.

I've got a cup of tea on the go. Now it's time for the Marks & Spencer scone I got from the branch over the road on Fargate. Spot of jam, a dollop of clotted cream. Just enough to sustain me for a session of snooker, not enough to make me feel bloated or sleepy.

I could be staring at my watch here, waiting for the knock on the door from the referee. I could start feeling the nerves in my guts. Think about all the people out there, in the foyer, on the lagers and G&Ts, in their seats early. The millions turning on their TVs at home, settling down for the evening. The cameras and the commentators, the table and the trophy.

I could, but I don't want to. I haven't even been to the practice tables. Then you might see your opponent on the adjoining table, firing them in from all corners, and you can't avoid the countdown, not in there.

It's messy in the earlier rounds. Waiting for a table to become available, because there's always someone who thinks that in the next ten minutes they can find the answer they've been looking for throughout the last twenty years. You get frustrated with the bloke who won't move on; anything could wind you up this close to a match, and you don't want to be on someone else's clock. You finally get on, and now you've only got fifteen minutes, so you start rushing your practice and stressing and thinking, is there any point to this, and then you're rushing to put your bow tie on and your hands are sweaty and your fingers not working and you think, fuck, they're going to be calling me in a minute . . .

So no. I'll sit here, have a cup of tea, watch telly. I'll use the first frame for my practice. If I'm good enough to win this thing, then one frame isn't going to make the critical difference. For all the shit that comes with the practice tables, I'd rather do without and take my chances. Let them all worry about that nonsense. I just want to have a good time.

Sky app on my phone, going through the channels, looking for something I can dip in and out of. Flicking about, settling on something easy like Only Fools and Horses *or* Storage Hunters UK. *Lose myself in Trigger and his broom or Heavy D bidding on the bins.*

Don't think I'm not ready. I'm waiting for the knock on the door. I might start pacing up and down, see if that helps. The further it gets in the tournament the more I pace around the room. I'm in such a hyped state now I just want to get out of there.

Every minute feels like two hours. That's fine. Accept it, deal with it. Up and down the carpet, big breaths, sip of tea.

Waiting for the knock on the door. Come on, come on . . . The rap of knuckles on wood. A rush of energy.

Bang. Flick the cue case open, take out my cue.

Pick up my chalk, pop it in the right hip pocket of my waistcoat.

A fist-bump with Robbie. Right, mate, let's go.

Past the grey breeze blocks in the corridor, the big photos on the wall from championships past. Strip lighting overhead, no glamour, not yet.

I don't like this walk. Some of the other players, they look re-laxed here. I don't want to be around anyone else. Just leave me alone.

People know now. They don't even try to talk to me in this moment. I'll talk to them in the morning, and when we're done. When we're out of our suits and shoes.

Now? It's inappropriate. What are we going to talk about?

I've got a look about me like a sign on a hotel door: Do not disturb.

I'm not this person at home. Only here. Only in these few seconds. The people backstage are looking at me now, but I look through them.

I can use this little dance to gauge where I am. If I flinch, if I show them anything, I'm not in the zone. When I'm right, nothing can distract me in any way. This tournament brings out the best in me, but it brings out the worst of me too. The thought of not being ready makes me feel sick.

I'm behind the stage curtain now. I can feel the atmosphere, hear the humming noise the Crucible crowd makes in the moments before a final. The nerves have gone. I've left them in the dressing room.

You hear MC Rob Walker doing his spiel. Announcing your opponent. Them disappearing through the black curtain and down the steps, the roars and the applause.

A second or two of silence. Touch the chalk in your pocket.

Twitch of the nose. A sniff.

Your name. Your roars, your cheers.

I just want to be down there now. Get in my chair, get settled. Get the ice in my glass.

Come on. Let's get started.

You play at the Crucible and you pick up the vibe from your first shot. This is the toughest place in the world to play snooker. You can't miss it. Not just for what's at stake, or all the history, although that gets in your head too. It's how tight it all is in there, how everything feels like it's on top of you.

The spectators in the first row can reach out and touch you. So could the ones on the third row, if they wanted. Even if you're at the very back you're never more than 20 metres from the players.

You can hear what they're whispering and you can feel the energy when there's magic happening on the table. An intensity, like there's pressure squashing down from that low roof, coming down the steep banks of seats.

It's tight enough when you get to the later rounds, and there's only one table in there. When it's the first week and a half and there are matches in progress on two tables and just the thin divider separating you from the other, it's cramped and confusing and absolutely off-putting, if you let it in. You're fighting to be the one that the crowd want to see.

Early in my time there, playing when Stephen Hendry was across the other side, you understood you were the sideshow. All you could hear was the thunk of balls hitting pockets and the referee calling the big breaks and the crowd responding.

You over a shot, trying to block it all out.

Focus, Ronnie . . .

Clunk.

'One hundred!'

Whole place shaking. Get up off your shot, chalk out, deep breath, start again.

Hendry commanded the place. He owned that entire stage. But that's the beauty of Sheffield; when your time comes, and you're the player they're all craning their necks to see, it's like being a surfer picked up by a great wave and carried along. You deliver and they respond. You keep delivering and the whole thing picks up pace and you skim forward together.

I've been on the receiving end of a few batterings there. Hendry, obviously. John Parrot doing me 13-3 in 1994, when I was eighteen. And those defeats help you when it's you dishing out the punishment in happier years. It's tough in there anyway, and you have to tell yourself to just keep going, pushing, grinding. Keep the momentum with you, keep the wave at your back.

Then you think, I've been exactly where the other geezer is, and it's a horrible place to be. I've sat there like him, barely getting on the table, hearing all those whispers from the front rows. He wants to run away. I know it. All those dreams as a kid of playing here, and now he's exactly where he wanted to be he is hating every minute.

It baffles them, sometimes. I've beaten an opponent, gone back through the breeze-block corridors to my dressing room and then had a text pop up on my phone. 'Can I have a quick word with you?' Two minutes later they're knocking on my door, and I know exactly what they're going to come out with.

'I can't play the Crucible . . .'

Now there's only so much you can say to someone in that scenario. Their head's a mess after the way they've gone down, and their world is collapsing all around them.

'Ronnie, I can play at any other tournament. I love the UK Championships, the Masters isn't a problem for me. And I come here, and I physically just can't do it.'

I'm always honest with people. I say to them, I know, it's tough, mate. I find it hard, too. It's one of them venues. You can't let the demons in.

But it's almost impossible. How can you teach someone everything about the Crucible in half an hour when they're in bits and you need to get out of there and have a good breathe yourself?

There is a secret. You can't half-arse it in Sheffield. You either grab it by the balls, or it will throttle you. That's the Crucible. You have to think of it as your tournament. You're the star of the show. You own it, or you don't. There is no in between, not here.

It's why Hendry and Steve Davis won so many titles in their spells at the top. It's why players like John Higgins and Mark Selby have been world champion on multiple occasions. A player either rises to it and learns to love all that comes with the place, or they let it get to them, and then they're screwed. You can't change how you feel about the Crucible five years into your time there. It's too late by then. It's under your skin.

I love it. Thirty years of walking in through the stage door, past the fans and the autograph hunters, springtime in the Sheffield air, and it's all familiar and it all makes me comfortable.

Since winning my first world title in 2001 it's always been this way. That was the year when everything changed, when I felt a massive pressure lift off my shoulders for the first time in my life. It might have taken me much longer than anyone thought; twenty-five years is leaving it late, when Hendry won his first aged twenty-one and Davis won the first of his six at twenty-three. It's a lot of wasted time. So it was relief, more than anything else. Right, I've done it now, done a tiny slice of what Hendry and Davis did. Whatever happens now, they can never take this away from me.

When I've lost – and it's taken me thirty years to win my seven world titles, so that's a lot of beatings – I can cope with it, because you don't lose at the World Championship by mistake. There's too many frames for anyone to sneak past you. When I've fallen short, I've always thought: you know what, I deserved to lose that match. The other guy played better than me; I made a fight of it, but it just wasn't my year.

You get back in the queue for the trophy, get back up there the following year, and then it all fires off again and you start flying. Each time April comes round I cannot wait to see the place again.

I love it, I truly do, in everything it brings. I want to walk through the door and make my cup of tea and get on a practice table. Even if I'm playing badly – particularly when I'm playing badly – I know that this squat little concrete and glass building off a side street in a northern town, up the hill from the station, round the corner from the town hall and the Peace Gardens, is where I want to be, more than anywhere else in the world.

Don't get me wrong. There's times I'm playing there and the expectation of it all can cripple you at the exact point you'd thought you were cruising. Sheffield has a tendency to make a match that appears done all of a sudden transform into a nail-biter. The atmosphere, the tension.

Sometimes, the bigger the lead you have in matches, you're expected to win the more dangerous it can be. Thoughts pop into your head.

If I lose this from here, it'll be a disaster.

Thoughts pop into your opponent's head: *I'm being hammered, nothing to lose now, might as well go for broke.*

Suddenly they've gone from can't pot a ball because the Crucible has got the better of them to cutting loose and banging in all sorts. Now they're only 11-5 or 10-6 down going into the final session, and you're looking at them with a mixture of surprise and resignation and almost fear. 'You little so-and-so . . .'

You have to trust in the Crucible's dark magic. Let's say they keep charging. Maybe they get back level; 10-10, everyone fancying it. The whispers going up and down the aisles and in and out the corridors. Ronnie could be gone here. It's on, the upset is on. And they look around them, and it wriggles under their skin a second time. Fuck. This is the Worlds. It's Sheffield.

Now the pressure is all back on them. Playing like they've got nothing to lose is no longer an option for them, because the jeopardy is back. They'll have to find something else to feed off, except they're drained, because they've been right down there and then come rattling back, and all the emotion and effort has left them knackered. Coming back from 10-6 down when it's first to 13 is like running a 5,000m on the track, being a lap and a half down and then closing it up with a sustained sprint. What have you got left now the frontrunner starts easing through the gears again? Not enough, mate, not enough.

I know. I've been there. Come storming back and then been picked off by a proper campaigner like John Higgins. After-wards you think, bloody hell, I was so close, but you're never that close. You've just been fooled by the strange ebb and flow around those cramped Crucible tables.

It drags something out from deep inside me, that place. It gives me hope when my game driving up there is miles from where it should be, and it offers consolation when it's another player's turn to shine. Because it's not always going to be your day, on the table or away from it. No one's a winner all the time.

In 2015 I came up against Stuart Bingham in the quarter-finals, and I knew he was playing out of his skin. I wasn't. I was scrapping my way through. I still fancied I might be able to nick it off him. When he rattled off four frames on the bounce to beat me 13-9, that was okay too. I wasn't thinking that he was only tenth in the world, or was thirty-eight years old and had never made a World final, or that my defeat meant I wouldn't be in the final for the first time in four years. I felt I'd got the most out of the tournament that my game deserved. I reckoned anyone else in the form I was in would have gone crashing out in the first round. Beaten in the quarters by the bloke who goes on to win it? That's okay. I've used the Crucible to help me, and the Crucible has used me to conjure up its drama.

These are the times when you sense that everyone is talking behind your back.

Ronnie's not firing. Bingham's not scared of him.

Ali Carter's gonna beat Ronnie. Ali's playing well. He likes playing Ronnie, he's up for the fight.

At the Crucible it's there in the morning when you walk in and it's there under the lights as you play. None of it might get said in front of your face, but you know it's going on. You can tell by people's reactions towards you – at the stage door, round the café in the lower foyer, when you come through the curtains and down the steps of the aisle. They let you get on with your business because they know you've got your work cut out, but you pick up on all of it.

In a way it's a privilege. It's a compliment the whispers and rumours are about you. It's like when Hendry went behind against Steve James in the quarters in 1991, when he was world number one and everyone assumed he was nailed on to retain his title, or when Ken Doherty started stretching away from Hendry in the final six years later. It's like when Steve Davis began to crack in the Eighties. No one is talking about anything but the scoreboard and the shock. When it comes off, the tremors go through the building – every floor, every room. He's out! He's out!

And it opens the whole tournament up. All of a sudden everyone fancies they can win a world title: the outsiders, the chancers, the ones who might have been fancied anyway.

I never wanted to play Hendry when he was flying out of his nut. Why would you? I don't want to play John Higgins when he's in the John Higgins groove. I want to play them on the big stage, of course I do, and there is nothing better than beating the top players in the tournament you care about more than any other, but you don't want to play them every time.

It's too hard. It takes too much out of you. You've only got a few battles like that in your body – maybe three or four across your entire career. I don't want to draw them in every quarter-final, in every semi. If they lose to someone else, it makes my life easier. And surviving for a long time at the Crucible is all about making it as easy as you can.

Durability is the key. How long you can hold the pace, how long you can keep the intensity of concentration. It's no good going off like a maniac, then dying.

Here's something we can all take from the lessons the Crucible has taught me. It's about controlling the tempo, whether you're playing snooker or out in the real world. None of us can sustain it in the red zone. You might think you can, but you can't.

We all have different thresholds – for how long we can concentrate, for what we can soak up. The effort we can pour into something. Ten years ago I could win the World Championship, with all the stress and pressure and exhaustion that entails, and think: I could do that again tomorrow. I was floating along on Cloud Nine. I thought I could do anything again.

Now, when I win it, I'm destroyed for the next two weeks. Like I've gone down with a virus or something. I put that much into them, emotionally and physically.

What's your threshold? That's a really useful question to know the answer to. Recognise when you're getting close. Look at yourself and ask another question: how is this affecting me?

It changes as we get older. When you're in your early twenties you can go out Thursday, Friday and Saturday and be good to go again on Monday night. You can light the candle at both ends and not burn your fingers. When you're in your forties, it's not going to be the same. You can still enjoy yourself in the same way, but it takes you longer to recover.

We all become battle-hardened to what we do. We can get accidentally fit for our job. Halfway through the Worlds, I feel what I think of as snooker fit. Someone who writes for a living can get perfectly used to knocking out 3,000 beautiful words a day, when that seems impossible to someone else. An expert brickie will be bricklaying fit, in a way I could never be.

But you will reach your threshold, all the same. So plan a period, after a big emotional and physical commitment, in which you can decompress. Work out what you need to be able to go again. Maybe it's sleep, maybe it's a change of scene. Maybe it's limiting your screen time or building in a week where you're going to get ten hours' sleep a night.

Know what you need to do.

There is a tax to be paid on any stressful situations you go through. Work out how much you're willing to pay, what this thing is worth to you. Then make your decision: is this really for me?

The first World Championships I remember as a kid are more the outlier ones. Not Dennis Taylor and Steve Davis and the black ball final in 1985, nor Davis on his calm rampage in the years before against Jimmy White and Cliff Thorburn.

It was Joe Johnson beating Davis as a 150-1 outsider in 1986, never having won a ranking tournament in his life, only winning in a televised match for the first time the year before. It was him reaching the final again in 1987, after doing absolutely nothing all season.

So many details still in my mind. The Embassy cigarette branding around the Crucible blue this time rather than the usual red. The way Johnson looked. The way he won.

Johnson was a Crucible player. That was it. He had the temperament, he had the game. He was comfortable out there on that strange little cramped patch of carpet – the long sessions, the jeopardy. When he got ahead, he didn't ever look back, didn't ever bother about the calibre of the man on his heels, waiting for him to make a mistake. Better players than him everywhere he looked, but they took in the history and the pressure and got a little scared, and he did not.

That's how you win at the Crucible. Can you block the bad thoughts from your head? Can you just play? Can you forget the scoreboard, become metronomic in everything you do?

If you don't know about the Crucible Curse, here's how it works. No player has ever won their debut world title then won it again the following year. Not the best who have lived. Davis got thumped 10-1 by Tony Knowles in the first round. Hendry got pumped by James in that second-round match. Hendry did me 17-13 in the semi in 2002.

Joe was the one who looked most like doing it. Ken Doherty's the only other man to make the world final the year after first winning it, and he never got as close in 1998 as Joe did in 1987. Joe was only four frames away, and he was playing peak Davis again. That's pretty nuts.

He locked me into what the World Championship is about, Joe Johnson. After him I was hooked. The thud he got with the white into the object ball, that good noise, that solid noise. I've rewatched some of his old games on YouTube, and I still like what I see and hear. He was a proper player. Nothing he did in Sheffield was a fluke.

It was inevitable my dad would take me up there, the amount I was playing as a kid, the amount I was watching. It was the final of 1989, the last session, the first day of May. Davis against John Parrott, Davis like nothing I'd ever witnessed before. I was three rows behind him, and I couldn't stop looking at him.

I'm here, and Steve Davis is just . . . there.

He was 13-3 up when I sat down. Five frames later and he'd won them all for a sixth world title.

Sitting in the empty Crucible would have been enough for me. Worth the long trip up the M1 and the early start and the late home. To see my hero as an actual living moving person was almost too much for me to take in. Everything about him was perfect: his crisp white shirt, how his black waistcoat fitted him, the old-fashioned watch on his left wrist, the middle finger on his bridge hand tapping up and down like he was impatient to get this whole thing wrapped up even faster.

I'd been a Jimmy White fan at first. I'd leg it back from school, stick on BBC2 and watch as many frames as I could before tea. I always wanted Jimmy to beat Davis in their semi-finals – the way he played, the vulnerability you could sense. The way he looked as pale as the white ball and about as wide as his cue.

I was playing the game then myself but mainly for fun. Then I started winning a few junior tournaments, and started liking the feeling of winning tournaments. The relationship between my dad and me developed from just being his son playing snooker to, 'Alright, Ron, we're going do this for real now'. So we had a lot of conversations about how it was done and who I should be. 'I know you like Jimmy, but if you want to be a winner, you've got to follow Davis, he's the man . . .'

Jimmy used to spin the cue as he hit the ball. I'd thought that was the way to play. I didn't know until we spoke about it years later that he only did it to slow himself down. Whirlwinds get out of control pretty fast.

So I spun my cue because Jimmy had done it, all the way to the point that I realised Davis was the one with the world titles, the one coming through all those semis with a smile on his face. From that moment on, I changed. I had to stop being

Jimmy. From the age of eleven, I based my entire technique around Davis instead.

It might have begun with his winning streak, but once I realised Davis was the man, the one I wanted to be, I took it all on: his mannerisms, the style. When other people would trot out the old line about him being boring, I couldn't work out what you could possibly find boring about him. He was playing the game exactly how we all wanted to play.

He was perfection. The way he walked, the way he sipped his water. Everything about him was incredible; how he chalked his cue, the manner he commanded the table with.

He had an aura. He was like the Crucible version of a supreme being. You had Jimmy, you had Parrott, you had a lot of fantastic players. A golden era for the game. But Davis stood above them all.

Then Hendry came along, and as you watched in shock and awe, he took over. The new gunslinger in town.

I first saw him when he was fifteen years old and I was nine. I got taken to a snooker festival at a club in Hastings, punters five deep around the table. He was playing a guy called Paul Tanner, one of the very best amateurs on the scene, a player who had won a lot of good events. I'd heard about this boy from Scotland before, and I'd read about him in the snooker magazines, but I couldn't believe what I was watching.

Tanner eventually won, yet you barely remembered that. Hendry was different to anyone I'd ever watched before: a new rhythm to his shot-making, a mad level of confidence for a kid. I went back to my mum and dad's and told everyone I could find: 'I've just watched the best player I have ever seen.'

My uncle chirped up, because that's the sort of family I had: 'Don't give me that, how old you say he was? Fifteen?'

'I swear. Honestly. You wait and see . . .'

I couldn't stop thinking about him. The way he had walked around the table surely had to be an act, because there was so much swagger to it. It wasn't normal. And then I watched him as he kept doing it, and turned pro aged sixteen, and won the Rothman's Grand Prix a year later, and I understood it was all real. There was an unshakeable inner confidence because he knew exactly what he was capable of doing.

Since I have got to know Stephen as a man, I've understood he's actually quite a shy, quiet sort of guy. But you put that suit on and you pick up that cue in your hand and you become a different person. You win five world titles in a row and there will be an aura about you. You will develop a massive internal belief system. It's not intentional, and it's not an act; it's organic, and it comes from within.

I didn't try to borrow any of that, as I had done with Davis. I couldn't. Hendry was too far out of reach. As I got older, I'd model myself on a Ken Doherty or Alan McManus, because they were the ones I'd grown up with. They were from my world. They were reachable.

Hendry was from another planet. How could I ever hope to be what he was?

And all this helps illustrate how hard it is when you first compete at the Crucible. Only very rarely does a debutant play well in Sheffield. Even Hendry didn't, knocked out by Willie Thorne in the first round in 1986. Okay, it was only 10-8, but this was the same season he won the Rothmans.

I certainly didn't shine. McManus beat me 10-7 in the first round in 1993. I was seventeen years old and fresh-faced and I got a gentle adult schooling. John Higgins genuinely hated the place as a youngster. He got done by McManus too, 10-3 in the first round in 1995. It took him ages to win two matches in a row. 'I don't like the venue, it's too small, it's shattered my illusions.' That was his chat. I was listening to him thinking, yep, that's how it makes you feel.

It takes you time. When you get on your first good run at the Worlds, it sneaks up on you.

Right, I get this now. Okay, I want more of this.

It's the only tournament where as a youngster you have a good run and earn some good money and your main takeaway is purely that you want to get better. Every other tournament you do alright in and it's all nice. You're learning the game, happy with the cash. Sheffield? Go deep in the second week there and you realise why you play this sport.

Sheffield changes how you feel about every other event on the calendar. Suddenly there is no other event in the calendar. They all seem pokey in comparison. This is the only tournament that matters. This is the one where it's on you – first two tables, then one, and all the eyes locked on you, if you're doing it right. You go through the trenches and you keep going.

It turns you into a new person. You win at the Crucible and you are a player reborn. You discover a fresh level of respect for the game, a new belief in yourself.

I belong now.

You understand what it takes. There's a point, when you've won the Worlds, where you walk into the practice room at the quarter-final stage. You've got eight players there and you can pick out the two that are going to make it to the final.

It's in their body language, in the little smile on their face.

They know. You know.

Some of them are enjoying all the pressure, the competition, the crowds. The quality of the opposition. You think, yep, he's alright, he's relishing this. It's a long old tournament, and if you're not enjoying it, you're done for.

Then there are the others, the ones with their coaches still at the practice table when everyone else has gone back to the hotels or out for food, and they're working on their cueing action and sanding away at their tips, and you think something else.

Mate, you're fucked. You're burning up too much energy. It's already over.

They haven't worked it out yet. At the quarter-final stage, the tournament hasn't really started properly. The Worlds start for real in the semi-finals. Why? Because if you get down to the last four, you've only played half the amount of frames you will play if you go on to win it. You've got best of 19 frames in round one, best of 25 in the second, best of 25 in the quarters. Semis are best of 33, the final best of 35. That's a possible 69 frames across the first thirteen days of competition, and a possible 68 across the last four days. Therefore, if you sense a player is done by the quarter-finals then you know they're not going to make it. The pressure gets to them, that's what happens. The Crucible gets to them.

The World Championships becomes a circus. Understand it and you've got a better chance of coping with it. Every person who likes snooker is zoning in on it. The fans are there – the regulars, the obsessives, the ones who lose their minds when they spot a player, and shove their autograph books at you in a panic. If you're the defending champion or number one in the world there are even more things put on you. Every word you come out with gets held up to the light and examined for flaws. You will create more headlines, make more back pages, be asked to spend longer in more interviews.

It can overwhelm you. You end up thinking you don't want to be there, when actually you know of course you want to be there. These are the things that have made me sabotage in the past, almost want to lose so it all goes away.

I am not prepared to sabotage anymore. I've done that and I've hated it. And the only way to get out of it is to create your own terms. You make it clear, first in your own mind and then to those pushing you towards the bad places: this is how I want to conduct it, this is how I want to live my life.

So I don't go to the Crucible and practise a lot. I might go at 9 p.m., when everyone has gone home and it's nice and quiet – sneak in the stage door, make a cup of tea, do an hour, go back to my hotel. I am not going there at two in the afternoon anymore or six o'clock at night. It'll be packed, and I'll get caught up in the mayhem again. I pick and choose my moments and then it feels nice. I've freed myself from the circus.

I don't even practise at the venue before my game. I go in there nice and early, put my TV on, this and that, nice and quiet, relax, and then head out into those corridors for the walk to the table. It's the Steve Peters approach: we don't need to react, let's just be more proactive. (Steve, if you don't know him, is a clinical psychiatrist. He worked at the high-security psychiatric hospital at Rampton for a long time, and then with Olympic champions like Chris Hoy and Victoria Pendleton. You'll probably know his big book, *The Chimp Paradox*. I'm going to talk about him a lot.)

You learn to cruise the early rounds. A player like Barry Hawkins has got the Crucible temperament. He's efficient, he's balanced. Stuart Bingham is the same. They understand they shouldn't expend energy they may need later.

When I'm playing well in Sheffield, I can steamroller players in the first week. There will be one session in the match where I might win seven of the eight frames and break the back of the thing as a contest. That's the efficient way to do it – get it done with short frames, big breaks, fast scoring. When your form isn't where you'd like it to be, the frames drag on longer and

35

take more out of you. Now the sessions are ending four frames apiece or 5-3, and you're having to fight your way through three tough sessions instead of cruising along.

It still helps, in the long run. It builds your Crucible pedigree. The championships when you've been forced to scrap give you an inner strength you can call upon when the form comes back and you begin to flow again. Once you've won a few and lost a few you understand that. It's a consolation when you've gone out early and it's liberating when before you may have been afraid. It's not the seven world titles that mean I'm no longer terrified about having a stinker in Sheffield. It's the awareness that the lean times help bring around the good.

If you're not finding pleasure in your snooker, then sometimes it's good to get beat at the Crucible. The intensity of the whole experience exposes all the weaknesses and private darkness inside you. All the stuff you don't want anyone to see.

Those are the days you fear the walk in through the crowds, the number of reporters, the feeling of being trapped in your dressing room. Other times I can feel more comfortable there than any other venue. It's my place. I know every corner and I go with that ebb and flow around the tables rather than being swept away.

That was how it was in 2017 when I played Ding Junhui in the quarter-finals. I felt happy with my form and good about myself. Where I went wrong was giving him a head start when he was playing better against me than he ever had before or since.

He took a 3-0 down early on, and every time I pegged him back, he'd then pull away again – 3-3, then 4-3 down, back to 5-5, out to 10-5, back to 10-8, then 12-9 and 12-10. That's what happens at the Crucible. Trying to come from behind five or six times in the same match saps the strength from you. Eventually you're going to make a mistake. And it hurt because everything up to then had been so much fun. I didn't want to go home. I wanted to keep riding that big wave and see where it could take me.

When I was early in my career and all in, defeat in Sheffield was hard to take. It used to leave scars. There are still times when I feel like unless you actually win the Worlds then they're the biggest waste of seventeen days in your life. I'm up and down. You know that by now.

But what I've only come to realise with maturity is that the losses actually prolong your career, in a strange way. I think sometimes that the gaps I've had between winning the Worlds and not winning have inadvertently helped me even things out a bit. To not get carried away, not get too excited. Three years between my first title in 2001 and my second in 2004. Four years between the second and third in 2008, four more years before my fourth in 2012. Seven years between number five in 2013 and number six in 2020.

Sometimes it does us all good to lose. You can't have what you want all the time, and if you did, what would you learn from it? How would you grow as a professional and a person? Being beaten helps prevent me becoming complacent. The more wins you have in a shorter period of time, the more likely you are to burn out. To become sated.

Every time I've lost in Sheffield I've driven back down south wondering how I can improve. It's kept me engaged and kept me honest. Even when others think you've touched perfection, inside you know you haven't.

Inside, you see only the flaws. You know you're only getting started.

1997 World Championships, Sheffield. Twenty-one years old, first-round match v Mick Price

Here we go. 8-5 up, 10 frames needed to get through, 14th frame coming up.

Could do with getting this polished off. Not playing the best here.

Long red available to the left corner. Might as well take it on, the way I am. My game in and out. Anyway, I'm a risk-taker, aren't I?

Bosh. Round for the black, little nudge on it as the white comes through to take it closer to the pocket.

Three reds off the side of the bunch I can work on here. Pick them off nice and quick, screw back for the black and the next red.

Five reds, five blacks.

Losing the white a little here. Bit seat of me pants, this, but let's keep going. Pot a ball, two wipes of the chalk on my cue tip, get down over the next one.

Let's have a quick look at the scoreboard . . . yeah, 40 points up.

I feel like I'm on fast-forward here. Don't actually feel that good. If I was good, I wouldn't have rolled that last red in. I'd have punched it.

Let's just keep going. Don't think about it. Don't get scared.

Seventh red, easy one below the black. Easy to get an angle on the black to go into the rest of the reds.

Pwfff. Bit straight on the black. Going too fast here.

There's a little gap in that cluster of reds. That's where I want my white to go. Fire it in there, get it trapped so it can't cannon off round the table.

Yeah, lovely. That's broken them up, kept the white close to them too.

Red will go left centre. Don't think about it. Thinking is bad. Go on instinct.

Straightforward black, a red I can roll into the left corner and get the white back on the left-hand side of the black.

Hate rolling balls in. Hate it. But I'm not on it right. I can't punch it.

Red goes. Black follows.

72-0 up. Six of the fifteen reds left.

Little stuns and screws to put two more away, both with blacks. These are alright. No problem, these are all good shots.

Two reds stuck together by the pink. Got to knock them out with the cue ball after this black.

Fuck. Missed them. But I've caught another red, and I reckon this will slide into the right corner.

Over it. Pot it. Line up the black. Don't think, don't be scared.

Let's have another go at nudging those two reds. Not too much pace, only need to touch them . . . perfect. Perfect.

Break to 96. Three reds left. All available. Black on its spot, nothing around it.

Red to the left centre. Screw back for the black. Black in, cheering all around me for the century break.

Red below the pink goes to the left corner. Easy on the black.

One more red. Bit of right-hand side off the black to come off the bottom cushion and then the right-side cushion. The red'll go to the middle, but I need the angle on this to come back down for the black, and I'll have to be above the black so I can get the angle to come off the bottom cushion and back up for the yellow.

Gotcha. Perfect.

This is on now. The 147.

They've stopped, on the other table. The one behind the screen. Think they're coming round to watch.

Don't think about it, Ronnie. See ball, hit ball.

39

Yellow . . . goes.

147 grand if I finish this off. Don't think about it.

Nervous now. Twitchy.

Tight for me, this green. Punch it now, Ronnie. Speed on the cue ball to bring it round the cushions for the brown.

Perfect for the blue.

Clip it into the left centre.

Frightened now. Want to get this done.

Don't look, just play.

Pink and black needed. Hands shaky. Fuck it, just dropped my chalk . . . Pink into the left corner. Left-hand side to get the white off the side cushion and straight on the black.

140.

So much noise. So much noise!

Here we go. One more black. Just one more black . . .

Five minutes and eight seconds. I didn't know it then. I knew it was quick, but I didn't know it was the fastest ever. I couldn't have guessed, when they told me, that a quarter of a century later it would still be the quickest 147 in history.

I wasn't happy with it. Actually, that's not quite right. I was happy I'd made it, but all I could see were the flaws. All the times it could have gone wrong. All the shots that I made harder than they should have been – the looseness of my positional play, the lack of precision.

Everyone else goes on about the speed of that break. Only I know the truth, or my version of the truth: it was only quick because I was out of control. Because I had so little confidence.

There's something Stirling Moss said when he was at the peak of his game in Formula One. Someone asked him: what's it like driving at that speed? And he said, 'When I'm driving well, it feels slow. I see everything coming – every corner, every decision. It only feels fast when you're driving badly. Then the corners come on you too quickly. Then the panic comes. The fear.'

That was me, twenty-one years old, at the Crucible. Perfection? Not even close. Those five minutes were about one thing for me.

I will never win the World Championship playing like this. I'm not good enough.

The twists and turns are coming on me too quickly. I'm out of control.

3

ADDICTION
KENNY, I AIN'T GOING ANYWHERE

I was in Holland when I hit rock-bottom.

We were at the house of a promoter. A man who knew people – good, bad, the ones who could turn you from one to the other.

It was sometime in the late 1990s. We'd been up about three days, I think. Clearly it gets hazy at that point. We'd been doing all the things you can do in Holland, pretty much uninterrupted. Loads of people in this house, and I didn't know any of them, and that was one of the problems, but only a small one.

Three days on it, in a period of two weeks where we had been going hard with only minimal gaps. The season was over; I had no matches to play, nowhere else to be.

Me on a sofa, looking round at this room of strangers, at the flashing lights, at all sorts going off. One mate next to me, same sort of state, looking like he was going to get up and go somewhere else.

That's when it hit me.

Fuck, I'm going to die.

I couldn't breathe. I could only just about speak. I'd long ago lost the ability to stand up and leave.

'Mate, please don't leave me . . .'

Then the dialogue went internal.

What the fuck has happened to me?

How the fuck have I done this?

Looking up at all the other people. Gone with the paranoia, but that's the thing about paranoia; you don't know that's what it is when it's happening, you just think it's reality.

So there's me, staring. None of them giving me a second thought, but I don't know that. I'm lost in my own head.

They're all talking about me. They think I'm some sort of monster. I am some sort of monster.

I felt . . . embarrassed. That was the next wave to hit me. All this? It's all self-inflicted. No one's made me take all that stuff. I've brought this on myself.

I've let my family down. If my mum could see me now, if my dad could see me, they would be so disappointed.

Staring around me now, trying to work out what time it is, how I can get home. Where exactly home is meant to be, right now.

I feel dirty.

I can't do this no more.

I can't keep ending up like this.

But I had no idea how to stop – why I was doing it, why I'd always start, why I'd keep going when most normal people knew they'd had enough and went off to bed.

I had a sort of insane method, in those days. I'd go out and destroy myself and then go and find some safe place to rebuild. I would always end up finding people who did care about me, friends who would instinctively take me under their wing and let me become a strange, wild-eyed extension of their family.

There was one guy called Benny who lived out in Essex – not London Essex, but way out east, on the Thames past Tilbury and towards Canvey Island. We used to go out partying and then all pile back to his house, fifteen or twenty people, quite a few of them characters in the wide sense. But because Benny was a tough old boy, no one would ever speak out of line with him, and so I was protected by proxy. He would look after me, keep an eye on things, and then, in the morning when it was all starting to calm down, we'd have breakfast with his wife and his daughter, and it was like I'd been there forever.

There were probably three or four different families where I did the same thing. Go off and do my thing, get messy, and then turn up and recover under their watchful eye. I couldn't go round to my mum's; she would always kick me out for that sort of behaviour. Fair enough. I'd get to the point where I was breaking, and then think – Ronnie, you need a few nights' kip here. You need a sofa and a few episodes of *EastEnders*. You need a cup of tea and a proper meal and a bit of Monday Night Football on Sky.

Maybe there was some sort of mad balance there. I understood we all need people around us who we can trust, who care about us. You haven't got to speak to them every day, but they are there for you when you're tripping along the bottom. Slipping into someone else's family has always been strangely natural to me. I lost mine for a while, didn't I, so why wouldn't I go looking for what I was missing?

I knew I was vulnerable. I needed those sorts of people around me. I needed anyone around me, to be honest.

Maybe if I wasn't so vulnerable I wouldn't have slipped in so comfortably. I've noticed that some others tune into it and want to make me better, want to mother me. 'Ronnie is lovely, he needs a bit of this.' I've milked it at times, too, because you can be manipulative when your head's in a state, but it is a real part of me. I'm a dog lover who lives like a cat.

The thing is, going out so hard like that was often such fun, right up to the point when it suddenly wasn't. The nights out you were expecting, the ones you could never see coming. The ones at home when you sat on your arse smoking spliffs and doing nothing, and the ones when you were out and about and the whole world felt like your playground.

I was out in Spain once, hanging out with Kenny Lynch on the annual Variety Club golfing weekend. Told you there were ones you never saw coming.

Now Kenny was a lovely man, a special bloke. He had amazing stories from his younger days about hanging out in Soho, years before Mum and Dad had their sex shops there, when it was all chancers and showgirls and coffee bars and secret mayhem. Stories about going to New York and writing songs in the Brill Building with all these musical geniuses.

We were in Marbella, this time. Early 2000, and I had a right old thirst on me.

'Kenny, I'm going out.'

'Right you are, Ronnie, where you going?'

'Out properly. You want to come?'

'Yeah, go on then . . .'

We were meant to be on the first tee at ten in the morning. It was 7 a.m. and we were in a nightclub when Kenny looked at his watch for the first time.

'Ron, we've got to go!'

'Kenny, I ain't going anywhere. We've only just started, mate.'

It's daylight at this point. Kenny is sixty-two years old. We're already twelve hours deep into this escapade.

He looked at me and winked.

'Ronnie, you're only young once . . .'

We stayed out for another two days.

Golf? The golf didn't happen, not that time. I left Kenny in some random bloke's house that we ended up at. Left him on the sofa, fast asleep. Gave the bloke some money for Kenny's cab fare back to the resort, told him to make sure he was alright, and then cracked on to the next bar.

There's always an aftermath with these stories. I turned up about twenty-four hours later. Kenny was quite keen on some golf by this point. I think he felt a sense of guilt towards the Variety Club, which was very Kenny. I asked him how he was. He said, no one will talk to me.

I had a little look around. Then I spotted him.

Max Clifford.

This was when Clifford was at his horrible peak. Everyone was terrified of him, of what he could do to them. None of the stuff that would emerge about him had come out at that point, but over the time I was there I got a strong sense of what he might be like. You could tell he was a wrong 'un.

I sensed that Clifford had this way of getting everyone to do what he wanted. He could take a scenario and twist it into a malign shape with him at the middle of it all, pulling the strings. He could crucify you in the media, and a lot of these people's lives depended on not getting in trouble with the media. He knew he had this power. So he was mocking Kenny, when Kenny was feeling ropey enough as it was.

I didn't care what Clifford tried to do to me. I thought, I'm not having it. My dad's in prison, my mum's been in prison, there's nothing worse you can do to me or write about me. Kenny is a beautiful man, and you're making him feel uncomfortable.

I told Clifford to his face.

Oi – leave him alone. He's my mate, and he's lovely, and you ain't. So do one.

Years later, when Kenny passed away, I went to his funeral. Everyone was there: Tom Jones, Jimmy Tarbuck, all the people who knew Kenny was an amazing person. And I thought about it all over again. Who I had been, why I had been that way.

It was all about escapism for me, those wild days. Don't get me wrong. For the first two or three years, I had an amazing time. I kept doing it because it made me feel great.

After that it wasn't fun. It was blocking things out, except it didn't make things better. It exacerbated them.

It turned me into a worse version of myself, and maybe that's what I hated about it more than anything else. I've read about what happened to Noel Gallagher in his caning days, I've watched documentaries about Tupac and Biggie Smalls, and I could see the same messy pattern repeating.

It's always easy at the start. That's the whole point. Then it speeds up, and you lose control, and it's like a car crash everyone else sees coming but you.

It's you who has to make the change. I had to get myself out of the spotlight, get myself out of the sort of bars and clubs where it would all begin, stop being around the sort of people who make those sorts of bars and clubs so alluring. I almost became a recluse, but that was better than the alternative.

I started running, I developed a close set of friends through that world, I went to rehab, of which more in a moment. I got on with my work, and tried not to react to every situation I wasn't happy with. If there's a conflict you have to defuse it rather than ignite it.

If I hadn't have done all of that? I would have been screwed. I would have been like Alex Higgins. I would probably have died from a drugs overdose, and it would all have been self-inflicted.

I was never naturally a rebel. My response to Max Clifford

wasn't me fighting the establishment. It was me sticking up for someone I loved, against a bully. I've always hated bullies. They're weak people feeding on the weaknesses of others.

But I often felt like an outsider, and I was a nightmare when I was at school. I wouldn't be told. There were two or three teachers who were good as gold with me. I could have an adult conversation with them. Then there were the others who would talk to me like I was a little kid. I could answer back, and I had a roll call of swear words to rival a docker. But I was never stupid, and I would always respond to the care I was shown. It was when they treated me like someone not worth bothering with that I would push back.

'You ain't talking to me like that.'

'O'SULLIVAN . . .'

I never raised my hands to anyone. I never confronted them. I just couldn't accept what they were saying or what they thought was right.

I always had to question things. I always had to stand up for myself. And Dad had always tried to drum it into me that it would be tough for me out there, and I'd need to develop a thick skin. All of it to make me stronger for what life might throw at me, and for snooker too, because that's where he wanted me to be successful. Nine or ten years old, and the messaging clear: one day you are going to be on your own, so let's get you ready now. The world waits for no one.

I was a blank canvas, as a kid. Open to it all. Looking at people around me, trying to figure it out. Watching what happened to them, constructing a worldview in this innocent head of mine.

When my dad went away to prison it changed it all. We would have conversations when I went to see him, or when he had a phone card; I would hear what other people said about it all when they didn't think I was listening. That was when the paranoia first began to creep in.

I felt like my dad had been taken away from me. It felt like it was all unjust. Me and him against the world.

It probably wasn't unjust. Not in the way I thought it was. But it became a team effort in the family. We're sticking together, here is the narrative, here is how we get through it.

That's when the mad seven years began. The benders, the blackouts. Me getting tagged as the spare Gallagher brother, the one who could match Noel and Liam all the way.

There wasn't the self-awareness when I was in the thick of it all. I was in the moment. I was trying to fit in a lot of the time, doing the things I thought I should be doing, as a bloke of my age with a bit of cash.

Clubs, girls, the sort of thing you do in clubs to impress girls. That's what I thought you were supposed to do.

I wanted to be liked. I didn't want to be on my own. That's when the trouble starts, for someone like me.

I tried to fit in, and my personality began to change. The drink and the drugs accelerated it. I became an unpleasant person, at times. A bit of attitude with strangers, like I fancied myself, and that was never me.

The alarm bells would only sound in certain situations. I would be in a club, surrounded by men I knew deep down were arseholes, doing things I instinctively understood weren't right, and something about the way they spoke about women always cut through the mental fog. The way they treated women, the way these women seemed to love them despite it all.

I'm a little old-fashioned. I hold a door open for a woman. If I was out and we were drinking and it was late, I'd make sure a girl I was with got home safe.

These men saw them like pieces of meat. I'd watch these

geezers operating and chatting and acting at being playboys, and it baffled me.

You lot think this fella is great, and he's a hooligan. A clown.

It made me feel physically ill. I'd have to get out of there, literally run out of the club. I wouldn't see that bunch for a month, maybe two months, until I got drawn back in again by my desire to be part of something. But I never fitted in, even when I thought I wanted to, not really.

There was a lesson for me, when I was ready to accept it. Be careful who you let into your circle. There are some dangerous people out there, and they'll quite happily use you to get what they want.

I'm so glad those days are behind me, honestly. I don't recognise the person I was back then, although I have some sympathy. I can see how you can be influenced, how easy it is if you get in the wrong crowd. I've noticed it a couple of times more recently, when I've found myself in situations and the alarm bells have been going off all over the shop. Almost panicking.

This ain't for me. This isn't good for me.

These people are not my friends. I don't want to be around them.

So I swerve it all now, when it happens. I am gone. You can see the confusion in people I meet for the first time. They're thinking I'm going to be a loudmouth. I'm going to be flash, I'm going to be brash. They spend a little time with me, and they can't hide their surprise. And disappointment, sometimes.

It was never really me, that image. I'm naturally a quiet bloke. I observe, I listen. I like order, and peace, and things that work.

You will never see me set foot in a nightclub now. I couldn't think of anything worse. I hate those places. I've probably gone into a club three times in the last twenty years. I don't want to be around drunk people. I'd rather be in bed watching a bit of Netflix.

I did a great deal of damage in those seven bleak years. To my game, to myself. I could feel myself in a downward spiral; I felt weak, and vulnerable.

I felt I was always having to push back against authority. Like I had no chance of ever beating the system. Like the only way I could fight back was through my snooker.

Certain things happened to me that I couldn't make sense of any other way. Shortly after my eighteenth birthday I was driving back from a night out at the boxing when I got pulled over by the police. Except not just the police, but every member of the emergency services available in north-east London. Half of Chigwell seemed to be sectioned off. There were five police vans, five meat wagons, blue lights flashing, sirens screaming. Men in uniform pulling my car door open and yelling at me.

'Get out of the fucking car! Get out!'

They threw me in one van, my mate in the other. Took us to two separate police stations. Me in the cells at Loughton, all my clothes taken away, wearing a white paper suit. I had absolutely no idea what was going on. That was the point they told me they were doing me for abduction. For kidnapping a young girl.

They admitted they got it wrong, eventually. The forensics gave them no choice, when all the samples taken from me and my car were processed. But something like that happens to you when you're already a little paranoid and already smoking stuff that makes you even more paranoid, and it all feeds into the sense that someone, or something, is out to get you.

Dad was in prison. Then my mum went away for seven months for VAT fraud, and it escalated again. Now I had a genuine sense that someone had decided my family were fair game.

These O'Sullivans, we're going to break 'em. The dad had sex shops, the mum runs them too, the dad's gone away, the son is a snooker player. We're going to put them in their place whatever they do.

Me, by myself in the house, trying to keep an eye on my little sister, not really knowing how, her not really understanding why. Going out to pretend none of it was happening, playing snooker to try to make it all better again.

That's when I thought to myself: you know what, I've got to toughen up here. I could easily go under. I need to be strong for my family. Everything I do when Mum gets out and she's all on her own is going to be about protecting her. Everything is going to be about making Dad proud. Making them stick together. Just coming through it all, whatever it takes.

It feels strange, looking back at the young man who felt that way almost thirty years ago. I've had to ask my mum sometimes:

'Mum, have I always been a bit dark?'

'No, Ron, you was a happy kid.'

I don't always like confronting the past. I've tried doing it before and I find it leaves me in a worse place. I'd rather skirt around it, act my way out of it, pretend I'm someone else. Find a distraction – go running, go to the practice table.

But sometimes you have to force yourself to go back. To find the way you were. To find the real you, before everyone else got in the way.

It's 1990. I'm fourteen years old, and I'm playing snooker on live telly for the very first time.

The tournament has got Barry Hearn all over it. It's called the Cockney Snooker Classic, for starters, and it's on Thames Television, which makes sense. Some of Barry's top players – Steve Davis, Dennis Taylor, Allison Fisher – against the next generation. Each match is a single frame.

My class at school are all watching back in the classroom.

The scheduled cookery lesson has been cancelled, the big telly wheeled in. I'm up against a guy called Steve Ventham, English amateur champion, one of the best that hasn't yet turned pro.

This is the real Ronnie, before everything else got in the way. And when I watch this frame back today, thirty-three years on, what do I see?

This is as good as it gets.

I am still not as good as this now.

It's there in the way I walk round the table. It's in my cueing action: back hand perfect, arm straight, head still. My arm doesn't drop as it comes.

The cue power is almost shocking. The cueing itself is so smooth.

Some of the shots I almost hit too well. Lovely angles off a red, drifting around to the blue, Jimmy White-level talent. Lovely hold on the pull-back. I look at the feathering on some of the shots, smooth and precise.

I look at the purpose in my walk, the little pretend yawn as I go round the table. I got that off Steve Davis. Acting like my hero.

So young. Hair neat, bow tie perfect. Old-fashioned cut to the waistcoat, scallop-shaped neck.

I look at how close my bridge hand is, look how close everything is. Bang! Everything is tight, everything is in a straight line. Nothing moves, nothing can break down. That action is sustainable.

I see the white slow and then zip away. It's like John Daly when he hits a drive, it's like George Foreman throwing a punch in the gym before Ali in the Rumble in the Jungle.

It's timing. It's a gift.

I look at Steve Ventham's face. He's an adult, on his way to the top, and he's being smoked. By a kid.

He looks baffled. He's in bits. It's the humiliation of it: who wants to get beat by a fourteen-year-old?

There's an ability to play explosive shots, and it's controlled power. I am not just slapping it. Everything is solid. Another blue, as I go past 50 points, punching it in, bang. Everything is in the middle of the hole.

I'm totally in the zone, totally at ease. It's all happening in slow motion for me.

I pot the yellow, deep into the corner pocket. Another thing I've nicked off Steve Davis, coming off the side cushion and baulk to bring the white back down. If I don't kiss the blue, I'm probably on for a century. But that's not bad. Break of 75, in my first poke on TV.

Now we jump forward eight years. I'm a man now, twenty-two years old. It's the 1996 Benson and Hedges Masters.

I'm the defending champion. I'm the player they all want to see. In a squeeze in the first round against Nigel Bond, four frames each, first to six.

They'll rave about this break, when I'm done. They'll use it as evidence that I could be the best in the world, that I'm nailed on to win the World Championship in the next couple of years.

I'll end up making 128, and I'll do it at an almost crazy pace. Chasing the referee off the table, barely waiting for him to re-spot a colour, getting down over my shots and banging away, barely sighting it. Genius, the commentators will call it.

And when I watch it now, aged forty-seven?

I think it looks horrible. I'm falling onto every shot. Big long bridge hand, jabby with the cue, bit loopy as it goes through.

I'm fast, for sure. That's because I'm not even setting up for the shot properly.

I'm out of position most of the time. Cueing over a red for a black that should have been straightforward, fuming and puffing out my cheeks but taking it on anyway.

I'm in sabotage mode. That's what it looks like. Kissing reds I should be missing, leaving too much distance between the white and my next ball. It's quick, and it's weak. It's not sustainable.

February 1996, and you can tell that I'm out on the town too much. I'm flabby under the jaw and my backside is broad. The waistcoat is clinging on to my curves for dear luck.

There's none of that cue power I had at fourteen. The technique's gone. I'm trying to play like Ken Doherty when I should be playing like Steve Davis.

I'm rescuing pots. It looks like I could sink anything anywhere on the table, but it's not from choice. I'm just out of position. The white is light and I don't have enough control over it. Chasing, always chasing.

My left foot is turned in. I'm sideways to the shot, no squareness at all.

I'm unhappy. You can see it. I'm potting balls out of anger.

There's ability there. It's just clouded. I can see I've lost the superpower I had as a kid. The way I'm living, the things I'm running away from.

The fourteen-year-old Ronnie? He can win the Worlds. This geezer can't. Short little jabby strokes, awash with anger and dark energy.

I can't actually watch it. That's how bad this is. It makes me feel ill.

I was stereotyped as a teenager. Because Dad worked in the sex industry, because he was such a big character. Walking into the snooker club, buying everyone in there a drink. Walking into a party, coming out with his usual line: 'Big Ron's the name, porn's the game.' And there were a lot of parties.

Stereotyped by the long lineage of rock and roll rebels in snooker. The one to take the mantle on from Jimmy White, from Alex Higgins. Kirk Stevens and his late-night pick-me-ups, Tony Knowles talking groupies on the front page of the *Sun*, describing himself – or letting himself be described – as 'the hottest pot in snooker'.

They were always looking for the next Higgins. The one who could be wild but could also win the Worlds. The working-class boy making good in waistcoat and bow tie. The flawed genius, the natural. Out on the champagne and buying all the drinks, straight from the clubs to the table.

But I didn't like the flawed ones. I liked the ones who did everything right. I loved Steve Davis and Stephen Hendry. I was fascinated by the rebels; they're always compulsive viewing. But I hated the idea of being one and I hated anyone thinking I was.

I watched John McEnroe on the tennis court and felt uneasy and awkward. I watch Nick Kyrgios now and he triggers the same discomfort. I'm shy. I don't want to get involved in the drama. I play down my abilities, because I'm not a naturally confident person.

I see what Higgins did to himself. I also see what the system did to him. After everything Alex conjured up for snooker, the sport should have made sure he had a pension for the rest of his life. He should never have been reduced to knocking on people's doors asking for a bed for the night.

Snooker is never going to be there for me if I ever need it. I'm pretty certain of that. When I gave up playing for a year after winning the Worlds in 2012, my phone went very quiet very fast. It's as if you become invisible. My true friends were still there, but 99 per cent of the people I used to speak to on a daily basis disappeared overnight. When I decided to come back and play snooker – bang, the phone was ringing again.

I'm always a fired-up character when I get on the table. That's the part of Higgins that lives inside me. I have to get into that mode to succeed. It's either fight, flight or freeze, and I'm a better player when my back is against the wall and it's time to fight.

It makes me stand out from most of the others, when most of the others in a sport that's about control and decorum appear to be deadpan and emotionless. I always try to be honest when I'm asked a question; I slag myself off, I question myself as much in public as I do on my own at home, even if it's often aimed at my own head as much as anyone else's. If I played football or rugby I'd probably be considered relatively normal. In the NBA I wouldn't even register. But this is snooker, and I can't always be a machine like Davis or Hendry. I have to get angry with myself to give myself something to play off. It's a controlled anger, and I'm in charge of it.

Some people seem to think I have a problem with referees. I have an issue only with the ones who are not doing their job properly and not putting the balls back in the right position after a foul. I don't like the foul rule in the first place, and if you then ask me to help you position the balls again, at least trust me. Don't ask me and then spend twenty minutes micro-adjusting them while looking at a freeze-frame on the TV monitor. I haven't got time for pettiness. I won't get involved. You do what you want to do, I'll sit in my chair. Take as long as you like, then we can all crack on.

In the seven-year spell of carnage and chaos, I wasn't being a rebel. I wasn't trying to turn the Rocket into a Hurricane.

It was something else. I had what I rationalise as snooker

depression. I could be demoralised or anxious about my game, and when you saw me round the table my behaviour would reflect that.

People would assume I was losing the plot. I was, a lot of the time.

Now? You spend any time around me away from snooker, and hopefully you'll find me polite. I'm not fighting the world, I'm trying to navigate my way quietly through it.

I would hate someone to feel uncomfortable around me; my friends are normal, nice, soft. I am not a win at all costs person. I like those around me to feel good and be happy. I hate seeing people suffer.

I am quiet and I gravitate to other soft, gentle people. I'm seen out with Damien Hirst, and everyone thinks it must be 3 a.m. in the Groucho Club and 5 a.m. kebabs with Keith Allen and Alex James. But Alex James makes artisan cheeses now, and Damien is the softest and gentlest person you could meet. He's funny as hell and has a lot of stories, but he's easy and warm and kind, and I love people like that. That's where I fit in, in that company. I know how wonderful it feels to be looked after, and I like to look after others, now.

The snooker gods gave me another of their lessons. I was naïve when I was a kid. I'm choosier, these days. I know that you're pretty much on your own, if you don't look out, so I feel lucky I have the friends I do. I work hard, and I want my family to have a better life because of what I'm doing. That's what spurs me on.

I've realised too the whole world is not actually against me. It just feels that way when you're in the middle of it. The authority figures I bump up against are there trying to do their job, and I'm the easy pickings. They might try to come down on me like a ton of bricks, but I don't have to feel threatened by it.

It's a game. They play their role, you do your job. Do the formal steps of the dance and move on. I don't have to get resentful and I don't have to feel like it's a conspiracy. It's only that way in your head.

It still gets me sometimes. I still think about just turning it all in, choosing an easy life, a peaceful life. Walking away from snooker. No more dramas, no more confrontations. I had a disciplinary hearing with World Snooker a little while ago, and was unhappy about every aspect of it. I got angry. It got into my brain.

I took Osho out for his walk and tried to process it logically. My natural reaction was to say, 'I'm giving up snooker.' The easy one, too. But I thought, I don't actually want to give up snooker. I love playing, I love practising. So, that's not the answer.

I went to my mum's house, plonked myself down on the sofa and sat there for ten minutes.

'What's the matter with you, Ronnie?'

'I've had a shit day.'

Then I thought, I can't sit here too long talking about how shit my day has been. How's that helping? I've got to do something about it.

I went through the kitchen and out into the snooker room. I played for about an hour and three-quarters, and I absolutely loved it. I put my cue down and my head was totally clear.

Okay, we're back.

It was a big old turnaround for me. Twenty-five years ago I would have tried to blot it all out. Gone out hard. Got pissed, got stoned, all sorts of carnage. Ten years ago I might have been tempted to have one drink, one spliff. I might have thought I could get away with it.

If you're lucky, and you listen, addiction teaches you certain things. The first thing it teaches you is to recognise it when it's happening. When it's about to happen.

The second thing is not to blame other people. It's your decision to start doing something, and it's only you who can decide to stop. It's not the fault of your parents, or what happened to you once. It's not on the people setting the rules you might not like.

Addiction is doing something you know you shouldn't, but being unable to stop. It's carrying on and feeling horrible as you do.

Some people are lucky. They can have two glasses of wine and then stop. They can go out in Holland and go to bed at midnight; they can go on a golfing jolly and not stay up for two nights straight. They can play snooker and not have to keep going for eight hours and end up with blisters all over their fingers.

I can't, a lot of the time. I'll have a friend stay over who likes chocolate, and one minute I'm eating two squares, and the next night I'm eating two bars.

It can sneak up on you. Maybe you're addicted to your work, like I can be. This is why I set an alarm when I'm practising. I have to force myself to stop.

Maybe it's your phone, can't put it down. Pick it up when you're talking to friends, leave the room where your kids are to spend time with your phone on your own.

Addiction is about recognising the relationship you have with something. Then it's working out how you can free yourself from it. To take back control over something that might be controlling you.

Sometimes the only answer is total abstinence. If I don't have any chocolate in the house, I'm not going to eat it all in one sitting. Once I've left it alone for a fortnight, I've broken the dependence, at least until next time.

Sometimes it's staying away from the circumstances where you might forget you don't really want to do it in the first place. The people, the places. Situations where you feel weak and vulnerable.

Sometimes it's remembering that less is usually best. When we're obsessed with something – snooker, new clothes, a relationship – there's a temptation to think more is always better.

So work out what works for you. Where your optimum is. I recognise now that I will naturally lean towards overdoing it with snooker. I'll want to practise hard all the way up to a major tournament.

It won't work. I'm either doing it for pain or relief – pain, to punish myself, or relief, if I think it's somehow going to save me. Instead it usually just leaves me too tired to compete. I've left all my best snooker on the practice table.

It's about finding a way to survive all those mad things that can happen in your head. Because we all have them. Some of us just take a little longer to figure it out.

4

LOVE
SETTING YOURSELF FREE

Don't ever think I don't adore the game of snooker.

It's June 2022. Six weeks on from the World Championship final against Judd Trump. The close season, a time to forget about the sport, if you want to. To leave your cue alone and get out in the fresh air and warm sun and forget all about dark halls and hard competition.

I can't forget about it. I love snooker more now than I've ever loved it. The nuances of it, the logic, the way there's always something out of reach and always something new for you to discover.

There's a synchronicity between how snooker works and how my head operates. That was me as a kid, always fascinated by certain games, always the ones where you had to solve puzzles. I got my first Rubik's Cube and I worked it out pretty fast. My dad and his mates couldn't solve them, and they found it slightly baffling and more impressive than me that I could do it. I remember them looking at me and saying, You get it, don't you? Then, a day or two later – You've mastered it, ain't you?

A friend of mine who knows about these things tells me he

thinks I might have autism. The way I play the game. He means it as a compliment, and I think he might be right. It definitely helps in snooker. You want to bring order to the chaos. You want every ball in a pleasing place.

I love the complexity of this game. Always did – the plotting of breaks, the competition. Now, at forty-seven years old, after thirty years of going to the World Championship each spring, I love that I've got to the point where I can make the game look easy.

I don't mean that in a boastful sense. It's an aesthetic point and also a practical one. I've had to find a simple way of playing the game. When I go from ball to ball, I want my white to travel as short a distance as possible. A lot of players will be forced to send their cue ball all over the shop. Of course you can do that, and sometimes you have to. But simplicity is mastering the cue ball: the patterns on the table, the lines, the way they provide the mortar as you build your break. How do I get to the most important ball as quickly as I can? That's the question I ask myself. I'm not interested in playing difficult shots. I want my white only moving a foot or so. Use your feel and touch and the lines you find to make it all seem straightforward. That's what I love.

I've always had good cue ball control. I remember one of the dads talking about it when I was a kid – Bill King, the father of Mark King, who's my age and from roughly the same neck of the woods, Essex-y London. Bill pointed out to us that Steve Davis was always in the right place for the next shot, only a couple of inches closer than the other pros, but enough to make all the difference.

It's like the way Barcelona played tiki-taka football in their Xavi and Iniesta prime. They never passed the ball more than a few metres. Keep possession, keep racking up the touches, no risk because they were always in control of the ball. Then one killer pass to Messi and into the back of the net. That's a little bit how I like to play snooker. Be patient, be patient . . . and then get in round the back and kill the game.

The cue ball control becomes a discipline in itself, just as the first-touch passing was for the Barca midfield. I love the feeling of having such good control of the white that no matter where I land I can get myself back in position and dictate the course of the frame. I used to love watching Floyd Mayweather Jnr in the boxing ring for the same sort of reason. He could look like he was in trouble and then he'd effortlessly slip out of it and take control again.

You can over-complicate snooker. The secret is being able to get yourself out of trouble with one shot. Mayweather slipping a punch, Iniesta threading his pass, my cue ball control.

I love this sport, and I obsess over its nuances. You can spend years looking for the perfect cue. When you find a good one it's like Harry Potter and his wand – you keep it, protect it, cherish what it can do. Sometimes you might be lucky, as a kid, and find one down the local club. Some ancient piece of ash left behind by an older player retiring or someone shuffling further on. The old ones often feel better than the new ones. As if there's some residual magic left within the grain. Maybe gone brittle, a little weak on the power shots. But the feel becoming yours, the idiosyncrasies and balance, the distribution of weight along its length.

My first proper cue was a Burwat Champion, made by Burroughes & Watts. They were the company, going back to the Joe Davis days, going further back to the origins of the game in the 1830s. The first professional game of snooker was played at the company's headquarters on Soho Square in 1922. Queen Victoria had a Burroughes & Watts table, they say. Alex Higgins used a Burwat Champion. You know something's special when it can connect Queen Victoria to Hurricane Higgins.

My dad found the cue. He knew it was good. Everyone did. The only way he managed to persuade the geezer who owned it to hand it over was giving him a car in return. An actual working car.

The cue was so long. Almost like a billiard cue. A big white ferrule on it, the band of metal that connects the narrowing shaft to the leather tip. We took it to the cue-makers, shortened it up a little, had a smart new brass ferrule fitted.

I used that cue until the year 2000. From the end of primary school to the age of twenty-five, and it was a lovely bit of wood. Had I lost it I would have been in all sorts of trouble. You can't just pick up any cue and play, in the same way you couldn't stick a stranger's arm on your shoulder. You and the cue become an extension of each other, just as your shoulder becomes your arm becomes your hand becomes your fingers becomes your fingertips.

The ideal length for a cue is 57 inches. If you're really tall – 6 ft 4 really tall – you might have a 59-incher or even a 60. My Burwat Champion was full size even when I was a kid. I was told I would grow into it, which turned out to be sound advice. But old cues need more frequent repairs than new ones, and every time you put on a new ferrule, which usually you'll need every two years or so, you lose a little off the end, because you're sanding it down. Now it's 56 inches, so you add a little to the other end, the butt, and suddenly it feels like you're killing this beautiful cue. It's getting older and more brittle, and the tip keeps breaking because the cue is losing its natural dimensions.

There are very few cue-makers who the top players trust. For me, the best in the business is John Parris, who's been making them all his life. A workshop in Forest Hill, east London. So as my Burwat reached the end of its competitive life, it was John I asked to make me a new cue.

I didn't touch it for weeks. It just sat in the corner of my practice room. I wanted the Burwat to last forever. And then one day I took the new one out of its case, this waxed, polished spear of hand-selected ash, the shaft planed and inlaid with four splices of rosewood, and started playing with it, and it felt as if I couldn't miss.

Power shots, subtle shots, side, perfect cue ball control.

Because this was a tailored suit from Savile Row. Measurements taken all the way down the length of the cue, its diameter designed for the way I play. Thick at the end, slim in the middle to give me the flex to put enough compression through the white.

You cherish a cue like that. You get scared of overusing it. You are terrified of losing it. You worry that having the butt replaced will destroy it. It's like a set of tyres on a Formula One car. Save it, save it, save it.

A cue can cost you £2,000 but it should last you ten years. I want mine to last twenty, so I have spares. Stand-ins. I leave one at my mum's house, in the snooker room there. Another at the club. My real cue will only come out four or five days before a tournament. I'll pot a few balls with it, rediscover the feel. Now I'm only putting a new tip on it twice a year instead of five times. It's a beauty, a Ferrari in a world of Teslas. It only needs to come out on race day.

It's always ash for me, never maple. Others swear by maple. They like its stiffness. Me, I need something I can bend. When I'm hitting the ball, I am creating angles. I'm getting the white to arc, to swerve, to dance. For that I need flex. It's just like a tennis player wanting the strings in their racquet at a certain tension. You've got a big serve? A backhand slice that's your main defensive weapon? You will have your own specific and minute requirements.

The weight of a cue matters less than its balance. The aesthetics matter more than you might imagine.

When I send my cue back to John Parris for maintenance they get nervous, all from the one time I asked for a new ferrule and told them not to touch the length. I got the cue back, and I kept missing a certain shot. It didn't feel right and it didn't sound right. As I sighted down the cue on each shot I could tell that something was off, but I had to talk to John for us to work it out. The ferrule looked to me like it was sticking out a tiny fraction, and that was because I'd told them not to mess with the overall cue length. We had to lose a fraction off the top to get the ferrule to sit right, and then add a fraction at the other end. John did the work, I got the cue back, and within three minutes of playing I phoned him and said, *Yes, John, we're good here.*

It's princess and pea stuff, on one level. Tiny adjustments no one else would ever notice. The cue is part of me, and not only when I'm actually playing a shot. The way you swagger around the table, how you hold your cue as you walk. How it feels when you chalk it, how it feels in your hand as you assess the table. All those little things combine to form your style. If I'm not feeling comfortable in that moment, I lose my edge.

The worst thing you can do with a cue is too much work. Another time I got my cue back and it just felt heavy. It felt fat at the end – not just when I was playing a shot, when I was carrying it around the table. It was like lead in my hands. Now my cue usually weighs 16½ ounces, but I suddenly felt like I was struggling to carry it.

Sometimes they think it's all in your head. Sometimes I think it's all in my head. But it was there, even if it was imperceptible to anyone else. It was messing with my flow.

Turns out they had added a quarter of an ounce of weight. Or rather, there was a quarter of an ounce more towards the butt than there had been before. That was enough to throw the whole balance of it out. I asked them to remove it, a fraction at a time, and I tried it again, and I was flying. *John, you've done it, it's great. It feels like a wand all over again.*

I had a great cue once that I had a joint put in – a brass fitting that allows you to unscrew the cue in half. Works for some people, including Steve Davis. Well, that was a disaster. Ray Reardon, six times world champion, coached me for a while. He'd always told me cues should be one piece, and he was right. You stick a joint in and it never feels quite as solid ever again. You lose the sound. From a thud to tinny. In layman's terms, never fuck about with a nice piece of wood. It's like the perfect Italian shoe. There's a reason why they make them with one piece of leather.

I love all this. Stuff that only a very few of us on the planet can understand. It's almost like a form of madness, but it's a beautiful thing, right up to the point where the madness turns another way and starts torturing you.

It was the week before the Masters in 2009. I was in the snooker room at my mum's, in there too much, getting frustrated with the dampness and the slow cloth. Not getting the feedback I wanted, hating the feel of it all.

Fucking hell, Ronnie, the tournament starts Sunday, and you're shit, and you're getting shitter . . .

I lost the plot. Took this wonderful cue and lashed it against the hard wooden frame of the table. Shifted my grip and smashed it again, and again, until it first splintered and then broke apart into slivers of waxy polished wood and creamy white grain.

I had two mates in the room with me. Both of them standing there speechless, me sitting on the floor surrounded by what was left of this precious cue.

For a moment I felt so much better. Then I felt like the most stupid man in Essex. Straight on the phone to John Parris.

'John, I've fucked it.'

'What do you mean?'

'The cue's gone. Send me down what else you got.'

'Fucking hell.'

'Just send them, mate. Stick them in a cab.'

Ten cues arrived. There's got to be a keeper out of ten of them, right? Tried one, no good. Tried another one, no good.

I looked at another one. It looked too fat for me, too big in the middle. I tried it, and I was surprised. It sounded alright. I thought, I don't like it, but there's something about it.

I hit one ball and the cue whipped.

Hello, what have we got here?

It was horrible over long pots. I was missing them by a mile. But in amongst the balls, it was nice. I could clear up, and the safety was okay. And I have to be good in amongst the balls, or else I'm done. Take that away from me and I'm a no one.

I ended up winning the Masters with that cue. I beat Mark Selby 10-8 in the final, and no one had any idea where I'd been the week before and all the mad drama that had played out in that snooker room. What an empowering thing to experience, winning with a stand-in cue you found two days before.

I ended up giving that cue away to a mate. It was never a keeper, not with what it couldn't do. And so began the next chapter – a year, trying out more new cues that John would send over, none of them right, me wondering if I would ever get lucky again. Trying another cue-maker, an old boy who just loved constructing them, who wasn't interested in making thousands out of it. Finding his best cue was okay but never a John Parris. Going back to John, getting the measurements exact, the feel, the balance. And when we struck gold, we both knew it. Ronnie, you ain't smashing this one.

This will be my cue now. If I play until I'm fifty-two or fifty-three, as long as this cue lasts, I'll be okay. I still haven't found another one to compare. I say to John: Keep your eye out for a nice bit of wood, because I'll always need those spares. But this is the wand for me now.

You never leave your cue in the car. It comes everywhere with you. When I'm staying in a hotel it will go in the corner where I can see it, either by the wardrobe or by my bed. Never by the window or the radiator, never where it could get damp. I never leave it hanging on a rack because that can ever so slightly bend it over time. I don't leave it on the snooker table at events because the heaters in the venue might warp it.

Actually, I do leave my cue in the car sometimes. If I'm playing badly, I leave it there because I don't care if it goes missing, in that moment in time. It's not my friend. That's my self-sabotage kicking in, my fickleness.

Some players give their cues names. There's a Layla on the circuit. I get that; your cue has character. You can definitely talk to it.

Because no two bits of wood are ever the same. That's what I've learned. I'll be out with my missus, looking at some wooden flooring, or a small coffee table, and I'll pick it up and stroke it and have a little sniff, and I'll say, yep, this is the one to go for. A lovely bit of wood we can polish up and steam and oil.

She'll look at me like I'm mad. But I know, don't I? It's my tools. My necessary obsession. Ronnie O'Sullivan, expert in dead trees.

This is what love means. When you're in deep, you find pleasure and satisfaction in every aspect of the object of your affection.

I've told you about cues. You need to know about tables, for this all to make sense.

No two tables are the same. That's the first thing to understand. Each one will play ever so slightly differently. No room with a table in is ever the same as another room.

Temperature, humidity, location of windows, location of doors. I can walk into a room and know immediately if the table is going to play well – the feel of it, the dryness in the air, the acoustics.

An echoey room means a bad table. Not for an amateur, or a decent player, but when it's your life. Anytime a tournament is being held in a theatre, you know you'll be okay. The acoustics tell you straight away. This sounds good, which means it will feel good.

One of the reasons the Crucible in Sheffield is an amazing place to play snooker is because it's a theatre. The tables play magnificently all the time. Wembley Conference Centre was great; Wembley Arena was good. Alexandra Palace is alright.

When you play in places like China, in Hong Kong and Singapore, the humidity is unbelievable. They can have all the air conditioning they like but somehow the tables just don't play great. At tournaments you can get away with it for a week. On a practice table in a club that's not in a great room, you're in trouble after two or three weeks. At the start the cloth is brand new. Then the dampness in the atmosphere leaches into it. It becomes sluggish and heavy. The slate bed gets cold, and you can try to put a heater under the table to compensate, but it's hard work.

One of the major reasons I struggled from 2017 to 2020 was the difference in quality between the tables I was practising on and the ones I'd find in tournaments. It was taking me too long to adjust. Then Covid happened, and the exhibition matches stopped, and suddenly I had time on my hands. I began travelling in on the empty trains to Soho, where a friend had two lovely tables in a basement off Broderick Street. It brought back memories of being a kid and going into town with my dad; he had shops on Walker's Court, Brewer Street and Windmill Street, and he would drop me off at a club called Ambassador's, where they had five beautiful tables, leave me there all day while he worked, and then pick me up for the Tube ride home.

In that strange mid-lockdown time, I would travel in three or four times a week. I did it for a month and a half before Covid delayed the World Championships in August 2020. And that was probably the reason I won my sixth title that year. For the first time in three years, I had put in proper practice on proper tables.

It was BCE who made the competition tables when I first came on the circuit. I struggled with them. I found they were tight down the cushions. That meant, if you weren't used to them, you could struggle to pot balls down the rails, the side cushions. I would lose position, start losing my precious cue ball control. I was forced to play rescue shots, and that did my head in. That's not easy snooker.

The first year I turned fully professional, they brought in Riley tables instead. I loved a Riley table – the size of the pockets, the cut. The middle of the pocket was tight on a BCE. You couldn't thump the ball in. The Riley pockets were still tight, and you had to hit them right, but I liked the look of them when I was down over a pot. You could feel comfortable on them.

World Snooker changed it around again in 2009, to Star tables. Initially these messed with my head. The cushions play differently. The ball slides off them. They play more square than a Riley cushion. I kept getting on the wrong side of reds, leaving my opponents shots. I realised I had to practise on a Star to replicate what I'd find in a tournament.

The sharper and tighter the table, the better for me. It rewards superior cue ball control. Tough pots get tougher. A heavy cloth is harder to play on, so that suits me too. On a lighter cloth players can bust the balls open, get back in position more easily. When it's heavy the white won't get there on its own. You need to hit it hard and with greater accuracy. The harder the conditions, the less likely my opponent is to clear up in one visit. If I do leave them in, I'm likely to get another chance.

It's still the old tables I love the most. The newer tables have to be made to a budget. The slate is thinner. They're like a brand-new car; they drive great straight out of the garage, but after a few years they're not so slick. The old Burroughes & Watts tables – big round legs, two-and-a-half-inch slate, good leathers – are like vintage sports cars. The ball comes off the cushion and sounds good. You're playing on history.

You're creating, when you play this game properly. Shapes and angles on these tables that others cannot see, flowing lines around the cushions. The cue ball dances and your hands and the skin and nerves in your palms and fingertips are what conjures this strange magic from it.

When the cue sits in my right hand, my fingers are light around it. You don't hold it like a man swinging a hammer. I'm a violinist with my bow. You feel every element of flex and groove and timing as you pull it back, play with the timing of the release, let it go through. You wait for that lovely crisp sound of leather tip on hard polished resin.

You are sensitised to the tiniest gradations in touch and technique. Should you push the cue back in your right hand so there is half an inch more of the butt visible, it will alter every shot you play. When your cue feels like it's longer than your body, the cue is in control of you rather than the other way round. When the proportions of grip and balance are right, the cue should feel like a toothpick. You're over the entire length of it now. Cue parallel to the table, so you can go through the white as if it isn't there. Hitting the ball with my forearm vertical, room to pull back and room to drive it through. You can deliver the cue much more aggressively, powerful through the ball but supple at the same time. A hot knife through butter.

You're sensitised because these minuscule tweaks make all the difference. These are the changes that give you a turbo boost. You might lose your edge for a year, try everything and it's just not happening. Then all of a sudden one thing comes and then you're up and away for a year, two years, three years. It's an easy game again.

Think about the area on the cue ball that you might hit. It's a sphere, so already we're talking a pretty small zone. A lot of people say you should always aim to hit the middle of the white. You might go slightly high to get topspin, so the white rolls on further after hitting the object ball, or you might go slightly lower to stun it – stop the white – or screw back for the next shot.

Well, I never hit the middle of the white. I want the white to turn. Me putting side-spin on it adds speed to it. It creates angles for the next shot that are not naturally there; it means the white can travel and travel. It gives me a power and an imagination that others might not be able to access.

It's the get-out-of-jail shot. It's the one you need a lot against someone of the class of John Higgins. You don't have to hit it perfect, but as long as you get the right spin on it, you'll get a good enough white to stay in the game until the flow comes and you get your chance. It's why I'll play in practice with a white ball covered in small red dots. That way I can watch the dots spinning and gauge how the ball is travelling – the pace, the rotations, whether it is skidding, whether it's turning early or late. I love the game, so I immerse myself in this detail and I relish it.

Think about the length of time the tip of the cue spends in contact with the white. Impossible to quantify, isn't it? It's a small slice of a fraction of a second. It's a click of the fingers. It's a stone thrown against a wall.

Except it's not, to me. I want my cue to bite into the white. I want that leather tip hanging on to the polished resin as long as possible. This is what I mean when I talk about compression. I want the white to hit the red heavy. It's not rebounding into it. It's stoving it in. The heavier the white, the more control you have over where it is going. Your hands, making it dance. Your nerve endings.

Davis did everything with a heavy white. Inadvertently he became my first, surrogate, coach, because I would study everything he did – how he would punch the cue ball, how he would stun it. There was no slapping the ball. Even on tricky shots his head would stay still. Back hand locked, not flicky. Everything in line, his cue and his hand and wrist and forearm all one piece, all moving in unison. Head still.

Bang. You would hear the thud of cue on white. A different noise to everyone else playing at the time.

The thirteen-year-old me tried to play the same way. The fourteen-year-old me was getting there. But cueing is the finest of arts, and I started watching another technique, and it infiltrated mine and sent me the wrong way.

Ilford Snooker Centre was the mecca of the game in England in the late 1980s. A big Irish influence, too, after a pro called Eugene Hughes who came over. Others followed, because Eugene was the elder statesman, and he helped support talented youngsters with digs and table time. One of them was Ken Doherty. Ken is six years older than me, and by the time he was eighteen, he was a proper force – good enough to play on the main tour, good enough to beat all the top players, Davis included.

I used to watch him all the time. The first really brilliant player I had the chance to study in the flesh. A prepubescent me was never going to be as good as the eighteen-year-old him, so I had him on a pedestal for what he could do, and copying his style felt like the right thing to do. In my head I was never going to be as good as him, so I needed to do what he was doing to improve.

Now Ken was very open-handed. He would hit the ball and it would sound tinny. The pots would go in, but he'd flick them in. He wouldn't drill through the white. He'd peck at it a little bit. (His cue, by the way, he got second-hand for two quid down his local snooker club in Dublin when he was ten years old. The same cue he was using in Ilford at eighteen, the same cue he was using when he beat Stephen Hendry to win the world title in 1997. The same cue he's using to this day. Like I said, it becomes an extension of your body.)

That style worked for Ken because he was so good tactically. He may have lacked power, but his safety playing was brutal. It didn't work for me because I was a different player. I could screw a ball in, power it in. And then I copied his technique, and I lost the ability to generate easy power. A bit like a golfer who can drive the ball 350 yards and it's effortless, to a man playing it safe with a three-iron off the tee.

I went from a one-visit-a-frame type to a bits and pieces player. I still scored, because you never lose that, but I wasn't blowing people away anymore. A game that had been easy began to feel hard.

That's one of the many flaws with self-medicating. Through the bad years – the caning it, from 1994 to rehab in 2000, the booze and the weed and up and out for three days and three nights at a time – my technique got worse. My stance got narrower. I was falling into the shot. My bridge hand was so far from the cue ball that I was jabbing at it. No backswing, no pause in the backswing. I didn't even look like a snooker player. I looked like a pool player, the way I was hitting the ball.

I realised something, as the fog from that dark period began to clear. I needed an actual coach. Someone as obsessed and in love with the game as I was. I might have made the semi-finals of the World Championship with that technique, a final if I was lucky. But I was never going to win it, and at twenty-five years old and in danger of fading away I was desperate to win it.

The coach was Frank Adamson. He had coached Stephen Lee, and Stephen Lee's technique was the best. I said to him: If you can get me cueing like that, I'll be happy. That's where I need to get to.

He was a lovely old boy, Frank. In his early seventies at that point, never happier than with a cheese sandwich and a cup of tea from his wife Loretta, sitting round the snooker table, re-teaching me how to play the game we both adored.

I think he found it difficult at first. I came with a reputation. Not everyone had realised what I had realised. Ronnie, I don't want to mess your game up. Frank, you can't mess my game up, don't worry about that, mate . . . It got surreal at times. I would drive from north-east London down to his in Bristol and work from ten in the morning until six at night, and in all that time I might only hit thirty-six balls. Thirty-six balls is like a 100 total clearance. Fifteen red, fifteen colours – that's thirty shots, then yellow, green, brown, blue, pink, black – thirty-six shots. I was doing that in an entire day.

I'd play one shot and he'd say, No, it's not right. He would sit down and talk and I would listen. At times I would have my cue in my hand, thinking we're going to hit a ball in a minute, and half an hour later he would still be deep-diving into dark corners of the technical world.

I learned to put the cue down and listen to him. When he'd finished, we'd get back to the table, I'd play another two shots and the whole thing would begin again. He loved to get me driving my cue, compressing it against the fingers of my bridge hand. We'd both go quiet and listen to the sound of it. Ronnie, can you hear that noise? Frank, I think I can . . . By the end of the second day each week I'd be in bits. I'd sleep that night like a dead man. The next day he'd let me play for an hour, just hit some balls. Then that was it. I wouldn't see him for two weeks, and then the whole thing would start again.

It took me a year of doing it to get back to where I'd been at fourteen years old. Twenty-four visits and a whole year of playing in competitions, because I took him to tournaments with me as well. And it worked, because I won six tournaments that season, and my first ever world title.

Frank died just before Christmas 2022, at ninety-three years old. I loved all that we did together. He gave me a consistency to go with my natural fluency, and I'll always say that my career only started properly when I began working with him, because I felt like a proper snooker player for the first time.

I wish I'd never left behind all of the technique I had at

fourteen years old. Sometimes I feel I've underachieved, in many ways. I might have won seven world titles, and seven Masters, and seven UK Championships. Had I not gone about it in such a roundabout way I probably would have won ten or eleven or twelve World Championships.

But you learn, as you get older. You learn about the thing you love, and you learn about how you love it. A coach like Frank Adamson – and Ray Reardon after him – gave me the science to go with my inbuilt instincts. Steve Peters has given me the same on the mental side. A toolbox I can dip into whenever I'm starting to struggle.

Here's how it worked with Steve. I asked for one-to-one sessions with him. That meant staying at his house up in the Peak District. He gave me a copy of *The Chimp Paradox*, and I read the whole thing in two days, which was ideal, because then I could keep firing questions at him: what about this, what about that?

I still read the book today. I have it with me when I'm travelling to tournaments, and it's like doing my homework, part of my preparation for matches. It's almost as if I'm taking my brain to the gym and keeping it match-fit.

It works for me because it's about not listening to your negative inner voice. The one that says to me, Ronnie, you're a fraud. The one that tells me I don't want to be playing, that I'm playing badly, that I should go home. The one that tells me I should be able to play brilliantly, every single day.

It's not about only accepting positive thoughts; you don't want anyone blowing smoke up your arse. It's about being in an emotionally neutral place. It's about not burning through your mental energy. Some people give their chimp a name. I don't. I just leave him in the corner, and I observe what he's trying to do, but I don't let it in.

I pick and choose when I use it. Sometimes I almost need to let myself go a little. To allow the emotions to escape, to feel what it's like to stand on the edge of the precipice again. It's like my Rocky moment: can I pull it back from here? Then I take out Steve's book, and I start making the little micro-shifts in attitude. Two steps back, four steps forward.

And when I'm playing, I still listen for that noise, as Frank taught me. As Steve Davis showed me. The solid sound of cue tip biting on cue ball. When I won the World Championship in 2012 I was cueing as well as I ever have. I remember hearing John Parrott on television commentary.

'Even the sound Ronnie makes when he hits the ball is different to everyone else.'

That's what he said. What I used to think about Steve Davis. And he was right, because I was actually feeling it. He was saying what only those of us smitten by snooker could understand. The best I've ever played this wonderful game.

Being the best in sport is about that combination of the scientific and the instinctive. It's about taking the advice of others but putting your own stamp on it too. Not copying someone just because it works for them. And it's about caring, more than anyone else. There will be things in your life that you love. Do them your way, and let that love shine through. Having something in your life you feel that powerfully about is a wonderful thing. Whatever your passion is, nurture it. Own it. Embrace the good things and the hard things it will bring you.

Love is also about setting yourself free.

I used to play snooker until there were blisters on my fingers. Chasing perfection, playing for ten hours a day trying to correct what I thought were flaws in my game. Blisters on my fingertips from constant contact with the baize, from the cue sliding between thumb and forefinger. I'd try putting plasters on them. The plasters would come off, so I'd have to rest for two days, and resting made me want to practise even more. I'd try all sorts to get them to harden up. I'd urinate on them. (It doesn't work, if you were wondering.)

Adrenaline is a powerful drug. It's the sportsman's version of crack cocaine. When you're pumped full of it you feel you could run twenty miles and come back as fresh as a daisy. The moment you take it away, your system collapses.

I'm older than I was. Emotion and passion take it out of you. I need time to recover, there's no way round it. It can be a really good thing to make sure you're in control of your passion, rather than the other way round. I see other players at tournaments, seven days in, back on the practice table for an hour and a half, straight off a match. After playing snooker relentlessly for the previous six months. And I think, Why are you doing this to yourself? You're not enjoying it. You don't trust in your game; you have no self-belief. You're killing yourself.

It's a powerful thing to be able to leave something special alone. It's like Eliud Kipchoge, greatest marathon runner of all time, knowing he doesn't have to kill himself in every training session. Come race day, he knows he will be ready. Have faith. My body will be good, my mind will be good.

When I talk about leaving something alone, it's not the same as pretending you don't care. It doesn't mean you're not striving for the best possible outcome, and it's absolutely not saying that you shouldn't put the hard work in.

It's about letting go of the outcome. If I want to win another world title, obsessing over it – chasing it – won't help. I'll have to put the hours in on the practice table, and I'll need to build my form, and recuperate between sessions. I'll also have to be content that all that I'm doing is setting myself in the right direction.

Ray Reardon had a great phrase for it. 'Let it come to you, Ronnie . . .' he used to say when he coached me. Ray was a snooker genius, in his own way. He was also one of the most competitive people I've ever met. But he understood that clinging on to something too tightly will only lead to broken fingernails and broken hearts.

Let's say there's a job you really want. Do all the prep you can for the interview. Practise your answers for the questions that might come. Give yourself the best possible chance. But take your pleasure and satisfaction from all that, rather than the final decision that was never in your hands in the first place.

Because they are often fleeting triumphs anyway, these things we think will solve all our problems. You win the world title and that night it's amazing, but the next morning you wake up and have bacon and eggs and go for a run and you're already used to the idea. And by the time you go to bed it's all feeling rather anti-climactic, and you start thinking about the next target and the next dream.

I know. That's a lot of talk about love. But it's like I told you. That's how it is, with me and this game.

5

COMPETITION
THE SLOW CAPITULATION

I'm twenty-three years old, and I'm flying.

It's the semi-finals of the 1999 World Championships. Saturday night at the Crucible, every seat taken. Me, and Stephen Hendry – the greatest player of all time, my hero, six world titles won and after a seventh.

I'm flying because I'm playing like I know I can. I was 3-0 down early on yesterday, then 6-1. Now I'm charging – back to 12-10 down halfway through the afternoon session, Hendry with century breaks in consecutive frames, then me hitting back with a 134, then a 110, and now another 70 to go 13-12 up.

It's pure quality, this match. We're throwing bombs at each other. No two players have ever made four centuries in four frames in tournament play. The 134 should have been a maxi for me, but I've missed the last pink to the middle pocket – didn't even think about the 147, never thought what it was worth.

Later it'll hit me – Ron, that's a £170,000 ball, what the fuck? – but in the moment I didn't know, couldn't think straight I was in such a zone. Just getting down and potting balls.

I've played Hendry here before. Quarter-finals in 1995, done over 13-8, but that was on a two-table set-up, not so much drama, so I didn't take on board the lesson I was supposed to learn that day.

Today I've got my hair cut short, parted to the left. Pretty neat, ready for business. Baggy black suit trousers, white shirt. Black waistcoat with a purple back. Hendry's gone short crop, the floppy fringe of his early days long gone.

The lights on the table are bright, the carpet a pale red. One of those beachball-sized plastic globes by my chair, the words 'World Snooker' wrapped around it on an angle.

13-12 up. Four more frames and I'll be in my first ever World final. I've just won three on the bounce. I can almost touch it.

I feel fearless. I know I'm dangerous. You can tell from the crowd, and the roars, and from what I'm dragging out of Hendry.

I'm cueing perfect, I'm getting down and banging them in. I just want to pot balls, and when I'm like this, I'm a nightmare to play. Everyone hates me. Why wouldn't you?

Everyone but Hendry. He should be worried. Panicking. But when I look over at him, he doesn't flinch.

He looks like a machine. No emotion, no doubts. He's still got a baby face, but he's got killer eyes.

Fuck.

Better be careful here. Look at him. I can't take risks, not against a player like him.

It's not that I'm tired. You kind of feel okay, in a game like this. I'm just suddenly conscious of what this all means – Hendry, Sheffield, the defining session of a semi-final.

And in this moment, I'm done for.

This is when it matters. Now. Not yesterday, not this afternoon.

I've gone toe to toe for three sessions. And I don't know it, but I've just bottled it. Pulled back on the aggression, started thinking about every shot.

I start sitting on the fence. He doesn't. My form dips just a *fraction, his doesn't. I wait for mistakes from him, mistakes he's not going to make. Put all those things together, and it's suddenly a talented boy against a relentless man.*

I've shit myself, basically. About what I could do, about how I should do it. 'Be careful' just got me beat.

This is what tonight will teach me. You've got to take the match by the scruff of the neck right at the important stages, right when it matters. Even if you don't feel like it, you've got to do it.

Kill the ball, master the ball. Play the shot.

There's nothing unlucky about my defeat tonight. There's no miracle in him playing like this, winning five frames on the spin. 17-13 was meant to happen, because he did what you're supposed to do. On his terms, all the way.

This is the night when I'll finally get it. I'll realise how to be a winner.

It's not how you start, it's how you finish. Keep your head, keep fighting. Be brave. Even if you don't feel like you've got the bollocks, act like you have. If you're not prepared to take the risk, if you're not prepared to lose, you're not going to win when it really matters.

Live by the sword, die by the sword.

Be careful? Fuck that. Go out there and seize it.

It's July. Baking hot in my garden, out on the edges of suburban London. A time to sit around with cool drinks, to watch other sportsmen and women put themselves through it all.

Here is something I've found to be true, in my years on the front line of sport. All sportsmen, deep down, want to feel they are the daddy. The one waving at the summit of the mountain, the king looking down on all below. When someone else is above you instead, and you're at their feet looking up, it nags at you in the morning, and it clings to you all day.

The trouble is, the sums don't work. There can only be one king. And that is the secret to all of it: the ruthlessness, the cruelty of competition, the intense satisfaction that comes with working an opponent out and taking them apart when they think it's you on your knees instead.

You become ruthless, when you're in the game. You want to crush your competitors. You want to, and you don't want to, all at the same time. You don't like the way it makes you think, but you're always trying to become the best you can, and it's your job, so you have to.

It's Darwinism with cues and waistcoats. Habits and attitudes passed from one generation to the next, the champions setting the standard for everyone else.

When Hendry was bashing everyone up, he was shaping me, and John Higgins, and Mark Williams. We ended up like we are because we thought that's how we had to play, now we were big boys. Then along came Judd Trump and Neil Robertson, and they looked at us and took the game on to a higher level in other areas. They potted better than us, they were more powerful cueists.

What did we do? Try to find a way of combatting it. You win at the top level by doing whatever your opponent least wants you to do. By finding their hidden weakness and exploiting it.

Sometimes the toughest battles are with the ones who refuse to give in, even when the scoreboard makes it clear they've got no realistic chance of victory. Maybe they can win this frame you're in, but you only need one more, and they need five or six, and yet they'll jump out of their seat with an expression that says, yeah, I fancy this.

That's what can ruin you, if you're not prepared for it.

Fuck, this geezer is hardcore. I've blasted him off the park all day, and he doesn't give in. He actually enjoys it . . .

That's a horrible feeling to have. God, it's a lonely place to be! The whole world thinks you're still in charge, and why wouldn't they? You're one of the best players in the world, in another classic contest. They're used to the sight of you lifting a big old shiny trophy above your head, giving it a cheeky kiss, tucking it under your arm like an old friend.

Only you know. You and the bloke in the other chair. The two of you, staring into each other's eyes. Each other's souls.

I've recognised a similar narrative playing out in other elite sports. It's Rafa Nadal getting in Roger Federer's head by bouncing the ball twelve times before he serves, tucking his hair behind his ear, tugging at his shorts. It's Rafa getting everything back, even the sweet forehands Federer is convinced must be clean winners. It's Federer getting frustrated and trying to finish the rally one shot early.

So you have to respond. Think your way out of the trap they've caught you in. You can't just hope to avoid certain players in the draw at big tournaments; the snooker gods will make sure you meet at some point.

It can't be copying your rival's style. If I tried to play in a manner that wasn't true to me, I would be shortening my own career by playing a game that brought no pleasure to me. It would become about winning at all costs, and I never want to be that way. To wake up each morning and live someone else's life.

There is always a way. That's what we all obsess over. There's a weakness in all of us – me, definitely, but in every top player. It might not be an obvious one, and it might only surface under intense pressure, but it's there, and you have to find it.

You look at the balls on the table but you watch your opponent's body language too. A decent poker player can spot when someone is bluffing. You play someone enough, in different environments and in hard matches, easy matches, and you work out their tell.

You might have heard Andre Agassi's story about Boris Becker's serve. Boris's serve was a massive weapon. That and his volleying at the net and his athleticism around the court, but none of the rest of it happened without his big serve.

Agassi struggled against him at first, like most people. He lost the first three matches they played, and Agassi was a great returner of serve, maybe one of the best. And then he noticed something: just as Boris started his serving action, that trademark rocking forward and back, he would stick his tongue out. When he stuck it out straight, he would serve down the middle or into your body. When he stuck it out to the side, he would serve out wide.

What a thing for Agassi to spot, and what a tool to have! When he worked it out, he went on an eight-match winning streak against Becker. He got inside Boris's head so badly that Becker used to go home and say to his wife, it's like he can read my mind.

I think I can do the same with a couple of my rivals. I can see, from the little ticks they have, when I've got them in a place they don't want to be.

You don't always want to use that information. It's like Agassi said: the hardest part isn't reading them, but not giving away the fact you can read them. You've got to save it for when it really matters – the tight semis, the big finals. And you load it on them until they fall apart in front of you.

You hate this, so I'll keep giving you more of it. Just like Hendry would. Just like he put me away.

You remember how Barcelona FC operated when Pep Guardiola's team was at its peak between 2008 and 2011? They knew other teams had realised they couldn't outplay them, and had decided to stop them instead. So Barca reframed the challenge. You can put ten men behind the ball. Fine. We will still find a way through you. Once we score one goal, we will get two, and three, and you will fold. The choice will have been taken away from you.

That's how I like to play snooker. I'm not interested in 0-0 draws and winning on penalties. I don't want to sit deep and wait for your mistake.

I want to score goals. I want to entertain. To entertain you in the crowd, and you on the sofa. To entertain me.

But you're never safe. You're never free of the dark side of competition. When you've done all that struggling and fighting and fretting to get past the others, the most dangerous place to be is the top of the pile.

You become so good that everyone wants to take you down. That's why. You become so good that you can only fall. You've created the monster that's going to eat you up.

I see it when I watch Virgil van Dijk. When Liverpool won the Premier League in 2020, their Dutch defender was the difference. You were a striker up against him and you knew, whatever you tried, he'd have you. Ball in behind, he's there first. Knock it past him, run on, find him there again.

Then he had his knee injury and lost a small element of top-end speed. He's still an outstanding defender, but suddenly all those strikers are fancying it. Instead of avoiding him they're targeting him. They're going round him, they're trying to go through him. I saw the same happen to Hendry, when he dominated. It's hard when you've been that good. It's wolves around a wounded animal.

You never lose your old reputation. Even if Van Dijk was bowling about on one leg, there'd still be someone bragging they got past him. I played the legendary Fred Davis when I was sixteen and he was about seventy-eight. He could hardly walk around the table, and I didn't care. In my head he was still a multiple world champion, and you always want to beat a world champion. I wanted to show him how good I was. I played him not as an old man but as a legend. When you're the best, that's what you have to contend with.

I say I don't like the world competition creates. But I also take pleasure from getting my head under a rival's bonnet and having a good greasy-fingered dig around.

Certain players and certain styles are going to cause you difficulties. It's just the truth of it. You're left with two choices: you can either let it get the better of you, or you can say, okay, how do I turn this around? That's where the fun and the buzz comes from.

It can be a simple thing. Not a rebuilding of your action or total tactical rethink, just changing the momentum. That's often the difference between winning and losing.

Hendry was pure momentum. That semi-final at the Worlds was him accelerating away from me. A runaway train disappearing into the distance. So many lessons I had to learn over those two days, and me becoming a world champion in later years couldn't have happened without it.

Let's say I'm in trouble on the table. Forget that – I'm not even at the table, not for long enough. I can't do anything about the pots my opponent is making, so it becomes a straightforward equation: how do I get my momentum back?

You have to understand yourself, first of all. I know I optimise my game and I operate better at a certain pace, a certain speed of play. My brain is linked to my body, so if one is going fast and one is going slow, I'm all out of sync. I can't get a rhythm. I can't get control.

So this is what I might tell myself:

Don't keep walking around the table, looking at every shot, every angle. Play the first shot you see, because that's your speed of play. That's your timing.

I'll force myself into it. Off my chair, to the table, play the instinctive shot. I'm not even going to bother sniffing around the alternatives. I'm going to keep playing the first shot for the next twenty minutes. Then I might start to walk around the table occasionally, but not a lot. I might see one shot, see another, make my choice in an instant.

Bang. Done. In my chair. My brain is catching up with my body.

This is what I should have done with Hendry in 1999. Hit him with my momentum. Take his away. Make him the one searching for his natural speed, his happy pace.

It works for me, playing at this tempo, because I'm only doing what I would normally do in practice. If I'm enjoying a match, if me and the other player are loving the battle and feeding off each other, this is the tempo I'll play at. It's the pace where the magic happens.

There's no enjoyment when I'm walking round the table making miserable little breaks and it's all hard work. It's not my speed, and so I'm just going to get worse and worse. Of course, my opponent knows that, so he'll put balls on the cushions, so we're playing a lot of safety, and all of a sudden the black's over there, the pink's there, the green's nowhere near its spot. It's all bits and pieces, and you're deep in it.

I hate it when it's being done to me in big matches. I even had it against women's world champion Ng On-yee in a practice game. She kept leaving everything awkward for me, and she led me 6-1 at one point. I had to change the rules of engagement to come back and win.

What you're doing isn't working for me, so let's come and fight over here instead.

In tournament play it's obvious what I could lose if I try to break free. I could lose the frame. Fine. It's the prize I could gain that counts. Getting back to my rhythm, my magic numbers.

My dad taught me that you can think your way through anything. He spends his time now living out of a campervan, always on the move, no fixed abode. Everyone says to me, Ron, how does he live like that? And I say, because he had almost twenty years living in a 12 ft by 6 ft prison cell. That life on the road, the one you don't want? That represents luxury to him. He hasn't forgotten. He's set himself free.

So I'll choose the shot and then – bang – change it all. One shot, get all the balls out, black in play, pink in play, white on the cushion. It's taken my opponent twenty minutes of careful plotting to slow me down and squeeze me dry, and then with one shot I'm out in the open.

You carry on doing your thing, and every time I'll respond by doing this. You might pick one frame off me, maybe two. But you're not going to stifle me.

Maybe it goes brilliantly for your opponent. The balls roll their way, this time, and they win the match. That's still okay. This is a battle for the long game, and you have just liberated yourself from the worst they can do to you.

Playing with freedom is almost my secret weapon now. I think it's what most affects my rivals, more than my CV or career wins. Deep down they might like to think they could play the same way under extreme pressure, but the majority find it hard. It's what gets at them over their morning coffee, what keeps tapping them on the shoulder when they're practising.

You don't want to dread playing someone. You don't want

them thinking they have your number. But it will force you onwards when it does happen. Hendry was too far out there – too good for me. I was just learning from him. Of the players to have come along in my era, it's John Higgins, Neil Robertson and Judd Trump. Those are the ones who made me realise: okay, just relying on my own talent is not enough to beat you.

You have to feel free or you can't live. When you come out of a big final and you haven't played your way, it's like you've been sandpapered to death. You're getting out of your chair to play shots and you can't feel your legs. That's how slow it can feel.

Get up, look at the table, absolutely nothing on there, play a percentage shot, back on your arse. No table time, no rhythm.

That can be snooker, sometimes. A very personal form of torture, every shot you play designed specifically to screw over your opponent. Your tactics only to get in their head and stay there and run about kicking things over.

You don't like this? Then have a hit more . . .

This is what all these battles have taught me, about life: be brave in what you do. Take risks. A prize is not worth winning if you don't enjoy how you've won it.

I read a book recently by a former FBI hostage negotiator named Chris Voss. He made the same point in a slightly different way: don't focus on what you can lose, but what you can gain. It can seem hard when you first try it, and it certainly feels dangerous, if you're not used to it. But it just might set you free.

Because we all need competition in our lives. Competition can leave you exhausted and broken, but it will also bring out the best in you.

When I was younger, I could be lazy. Snooker came easy; money was there. When I reached the top few, I was pushed so hard it moulded me into something else. It built up an unexpected strength within, a resilience – to never quit, to always give your best. To shake hands at the end of it all and be proud of all you had given.

I became a better player after that blitz from Hendry. I owe some of my longevity and renewed vigour to the excellence of John Higgins.

These are all opponents who want to ruin your day. But they're also allies, in a weird way. We've all helped each other by trying to dismantle each other. How can you come to believe you're unbreakable if you've never been pushed to breaking point?

Like I said, it's a long game, snooker. Which brings us to the slow capitulation. I see young players come along all guns blazing, thinking they're the dog's nuts, thinking it's easy as they chalk up a few wins over me. I actually enjoy that part, because I know what's coming next. A few years in, they take a few hits. A couple of surprise defeats, where they can't quite work out what just happened. You can see the doubt get to work on them. I watch them slowly unravelling, and I recognise exactly what's going on.

I'm aware that might sound cruel. It's not meant to be. It's just the way it is, in elite sport. You might not have known you signed up to it, but it will change you, and you'd better get used to it.

I can also empathise when I see the same players try even harder to get back to the top, not realising there's no way back to the top, that it's just going to get worse for them.

What I know and they don't yet is that their methodology is not sustainable. They don't realise at the time, because at the beginning it's always easy. You're on the up escalator in life. Every day is a joy, every practice session and tournament.

Maybe they'll get two or three years of that. If they're fortunate, they could get five or six years deep.

Doesn't matter. You can't keep it going, because the effort you're putting in is too great. You can't play with such intensity in the long term. And if you haven't figured it out, and found an alternative way to win, it starts to eat away at you. You question everything you're doing.

It's not the mid-ranked players it happens to. When they have their moment in the sun it's a lovely thing to witness. There's not the expectation it'll last, and it's done with grace and an acceptance of the inevitable slide back down.

It's the better players with all the shots. Someone who will tell the world their game is good, and they can compete with the best, that it's only a matter of time until they win the World Championships. They believe it; they don't know anything different.

You listen to the big statements, and you wait. Gradually they get put in their place – not just by me, but by other elite players. They get taken to school by Higgins, or Trump gives them a few good hammerings. The bolshie dialogue changes. Now it's all, you know what, so-and-so is actually a great player.

Then it's the next rank of soldiers who come at you. The ones on tour who are really hungry. They're going to be out there fighting and they're going to play long matches and they don't care.

You're going to have to scrape me off the table.

It's just a matter of time. There are too many good players out there for you to keep riding that escalator forever. The moment will come when someone shoves you off, and then someone else, and someone else again.

They capitulate, but it's a slow capitulation. And that's the element you only understand if you've lived this mad life.

97

You come to realise it will never be easy, and it's never just about potting balls. It's about being able to deal with the pressure on a consistent basis, tournament after tournament, year after year. It's about getting back up off the floor.

I see it as a pedigree sort of thing. Can you reinvent yourself? That's what makes you last.

Me and Higgins and Williams, we've knocked lumps out of each other for years. We've accidentally made each other stronger. We're all in the same time zone with our careers. We've found a way out of the slow capitulation.

Competition can mess you up, if you let it. The rival who keeps getting the better of you starts living in your head. And you can feel this great wave of resentment towards them – a dislike, at first, then a blame, for the way they're making you feel, then an anger, as you find yourself turning into the sort of person you don't want to be.

You can't stay in that place. You can't walk around each day with all that negative energy dragging along behind you. It's not helping you in any way when you come up against that opponent on the table, and it's bleeding into every part of your life. As a mate of mine from rehab used to say, you're pissing in your own pants. And when you piss in your own pants, it's you sitting in that mess for the rest of the day.

So you have to work on it. Admit, first of all, that this situation is bothering you. Then look at it from another angle. Where is this resentment coming from? What part am I unwittingly playing in all this? Because it's often our own flaws that are contributing to that resentment.

I'm no saint. I've felt the seven deadly sins inside me. I have to work out why this particular rival has got into my head. Is it in part because of my own insecurities about the flaws of my game, or my jealousy at how well they might be playing? Is it greed, that they're beating me to these big prize pots?

Own the resentment. Reframe it. If you don't want to be that greedy insecure person, work on it. Sometimes I've had to make an apology to someone, even when my instinct told me it was all their fault. But by cleaning your side of the street, you help release that negative energy. Don't keep spewing out anger. It never helps. Don't piss your own pants.

We're all searchers, us top players. There's some, like Hendry, with incredible mental strength. Then there's others, like me, who are driven by doubt, to a certain extent. We worry the other big players are the ones who have the answer.

Because this is what competition does to you. Darwinism with cues and smart shoes.

When you're at the top, you can only look down, and you might not like what you see. The rest of them are targeting you now. The ones you like, the ones you never speak to, the ones you fear.

A pack of wolves, smelling blood in the snow.

6

ANXIETY
A SEARCHING MORAL
INVENTORY OF OURSELVES

We're back in front of the mirror. Looking at me looking back at myself.

Me as September comes around, and the new season begins. Looking for answers. Thinking about what's inside my head, and why it's there.

I feel like a loner, some of the time. There, I've said it.

I don't know exactly where it comes from. I'm on the road a lot, travelling between tournaments, in hotel rooms in towns that aren't home, and that must be part of it. I've realised how good it feels having people around you, and how hard it is to deal with when they are taken away from you. That's happened to me – not just with my dad, not just with my mum, but with other people who have come into my life, made an impact on who I am and what I do. Only when they go do you understand how dependent on them you had become.

When they are taken away it's like a physical injury.

Fuck, this hurts . . .

That's the definition of loneliness, in my head. The awareness that I'm on my own, really, most of the time.

There's a distinction between anxiety and depression, in my experience of them. Anxiety is when I feel trapped by fear. I feel I physically can't move. I want to lock myself away in a room because I just can't get the words out, I can't express myself. Depression for me is when I'm down and the world is a hard place, but I'm able to tell people about it. I can still get my words out.

My mental health issues tend more towards anxiety than depression. It feels like everything is coming crashing in on me. I lose the ability to look at issues individually and deal with them logically; they snowball, and I get frozen.

I can't deal with anything. I end up wanting to hide away somewhere safe, whether that's at my mum's house or at home, whether that's on the snooker table on my own or in my hotel room when I am at a tournament.

But then, playing snooker every day with nothing else in my life got me sick and tired of playing snooker. I didn't hate it, I just felt numb. I had no feelings.

That's no way to live your life, believe me. But those feelings come from caring about things, about my snooker and the people around me and what sort of person I am, which leads to a conundrum. I don't want to be full of anxiety and I don't want to be numb. So what do I do?

Here's how I'm trying to live my life, now. I search for the somewhere in between. I have a friend, Kevin Dutton, who is a leading psychologist – an expert in psychopathy, a man with all manner of good insights. He said to me, Ronnie, it's like having a dimmer switch on your life that you can play around with.

I found that analogy so useful. I can never turn my head off. I don't want to; it's me, and numbness is never the answer. But I never want to let it go full blast, because it's too much. It overwhelms me.

The last time I had the anxiety really bad was at the Hong Kong Masters in July 2017. I got to the hotel and felt in a really good place – okay, not the best place, but able to play, able to talk. They have a big opening party at the event – the players, the sponsors, some random bigwigs. About half an hour before it was due to start, I felt the anxiety coming on. The thoughts started chasing themselves round my brain.

I've got to go to a room full of people.

I don't feel good.

I can't get out of this.

I forced myself to walk in.

Take a drink off the tray, Ronnie. Nod. Smile.

Thinking, I'll have to spend at least an hour in here, just to be polite. Thinking, What do I say to this person? Unable to concentrate on anything else but the idea of running out of there. Sweating, pulse battering along, chest tight.

So I cracked. Back to my room, slamming the door, locking it behind me.

I texted a mate who'd travelled out with me. Look, I know we're in Hong Kong, but I need some of my tablets, do you know anyone that can get them for me?

He was hesitant. I could tell. Fair enough – when someone's begging you to get them some pills, you maybe think you shouldn't be encouraging them. So I phoned Laila, back in north-east London, and she was good as gold. Got in contact with my doctor, got the brand name and the dose, talked to my mate. He went out and got them for me. Within twenty minutes of swallowing the first one, I could feel the fear ebbing away. An hour in and I could leave the room. I ended up taking them for three days, and after that I didn't need to take any more, because I felt okay again. Free of the manacles.

I know when it's coming now. I can pretty much feel the exact moment it kicks in. And when it does, it's almost like having a cricked neck. Do nothing about it and you're struggling to move. Go down the chiropractor and he gives you a little crack crack crack, and within two days you're moving about again.

It maybe happens once a year to me these days, twice if I'm unlucky or not across it. It's brought on by certain situations, and I have to remember what they might be and when they might come along. The World Championships is one of them. If I let it happen, the Worlds will very quickly push me to the point where I'm asking myself if I can genuinely go through this anymore. All the other tournaments, possibly bar the Masters, it's a bit of fun, in and out, under the radar. No one really gives a monkey's, and that's nice and easy for me.

I set a reminder on my phone. World Championships: take your anxiety pills from the minute the tournament starts to the end. The safest thing for me to do – except in 2022 I forgot to do it.

My mate Robbie – the one who stays with me in Sheffield – saw I was having a bit of a wobbly.

'Ronnie, why don't you take a pill?'

'Fuck, you're right . . .'

And it worked. On them for three days, pushing the stress and the pressure back out to arm's length.

It calms everything down. Takes away the racing heart, the sweating, the fear. All of a sudden you can have a conversation. You can express yourself.

It's the snooker that is generally the trigger. Actually, not the snooker, but feeling scared about my snooker. Worrying my game is falling apart.

I don't have those strange nightmares you might imagine, like I'm walking towards my cue and I can't pick it up, or I'm trying to get to the table and it's like I'm on a treadmill and can't move. I have dreams that could be real, to me. Coming to the table and not being able to play.

A dream that stayed in my thoughts when I was awake. I could be playing well, and I found it impossible to enjoy it or to stay in the moment. Instead, it would be, how much longer can I keep this going for? And when I was playing badly, I couldn't switch it round. I didn't assume the run would break. I thought it would last.

I will be shit forever.

That was the waking nightmare. I never had any confidence in myself. It was pain or relief – relief that it was still okay, when it was; pain, when it wasn't. A self-fulfilling prophecy, a player fated to be inconsistent and unable to work out why.

And between the age of eighteen and twenty-five, when I was in my messed-up time – when there was no dimmer switch, when everything was always turned up to full blast – it was always the worst at the Worlds. Starting the tournament with everyone talking me up, me convinced they were clueless because, fuck, I'm the sort of player who can only play well for four days, and we've got seventeen on our hands here.

I was beaten even as we began. The same self-perpetuating negative thoughts going round and round and round. Day six, day seven, chances are I'm going to be playing shit. I always play shit when it matters. Starting to play badly and falling into the embrace – this is a waste of time here, I'm going to get beat anyway . . .

I didn't have the mental skills at that stage in my life to bite down on the gumshield and get through those blows. To ease through the early rounds and stay focused on the contest I was in, and the session, and frame, and shot.

It was only when I began working with Steve in 2011, aged thirty-five, that I began to challenge those beliefs – to resist the urge to sabotage, to say to myself, let's just go with what we've got here, get any sort of win, not worry about the manner of it. To let tomorrow be another day.

I've talked about taming the chimp. Sitting him in the corner, letting him chatter away with all his negative stuff, but ignoring it all. I'll talk more about self-sabotage, and how we worked on that.

But there was one question he used to ask me that still comes up today, and still works: 'Ronnie, what do you want from snooker?'

I'd never considered it in such simple terms. I just gave snooker everything it wanted, and let it control me. And when I thought about what Steve had asked, the answers came out just as easy and uncomplicated.

'I want to enjoy playing. I want to be happy. I want to take pleasure from my game.'

'Great, so that's what you're going to do. All the other stuff that gets in the way we're going to ignore. We won't let it mess us up.'

Gradually, over the next few years, I found out there really was another way. I could go into tournaments not playing well and yet it would slowly come good. From that, I worried less about it going wrong, so therefore it didn't. I'd just think, Okay, we can win playing bad, you've just got to apply yourself a bit more.

Maybe ask yourself the same simple question. What do I want from this job? What do I want this relationship to be? Once you've got the answer, strip away all the other stuff. You have your focus now.

The people thing, the loneliness? That's something I'm still working on.

I'm not good at being on my own. Steve's told me I'm better

with someone I trust around me, and I think he might be right, but you're on your own when you play snooker. You're often on your own when you're running. When I do my paintings, the dot style that Damian has taught me – that's a solo pursuit too. I've become accustomed to thinking that at some point I will probably end up on my own. From that follows the next idea: I've got to get comfortable with living that life, because I don't want to rely on anyone.

I'm worried the people I care about will leave. Flurries of panic – what if I get reliant on them, and they're taken away, and oh fuck, again. I tell myself to be careful how much I invest in others, because what am I truly without them? To try not to be too dependent on anyone, or anything – a job, a person, a place. If they are taken away from you, where does that leave you?

Maybe that's the definition of love. It's the high-wire act. You have to commit yourself totally to make it work, but if it fails, it's an awful long way down. It scares me to think about it. Perhaps I'm not really ready to go there.

I find engaging with social media triggers the anxiety. If I wasn't playing snooker for a living, maybe I could scroll Twitter, I could flick around on WhatsApp. But I find when I do that my brain becomes flitty, and I feel like I've got to get back to this person, get back to that person, follow up on a new group I've been added to. My job is to play snooker. To do that I must have a clear mind. When I'm scrolling, it's taking me in the opposite direction. Most of us thrive on peace and simplicity. The more we incorporate those into our lives, the better a place we're in.

I've never been on Facebook. I joined WhatsApp because my dad was away and wanted to send me messages and photos, but I could feel it sucking me in, so I deleted it when he came back.

I joined Instagram when a friend told me it would be good for business if I could post stories, and within a week my head was a mess. As soon as I ditched it, I felt significantly better. Twitter? I had my kids for the weekend a little while ago, and I got into an argument with another snooker player on it and was lost for three hours. It felt so wrong.

These, then, are some of the mental issues I battle with. And this is the clarity I have found around them, in the last few years: I know I want to play snooker, and I know I love it, and I never really want to give it up. In order to keep playing, I've had to find ways to manage my life, my emotions and my time. I've had to control the dimmer switch.

Going to rehab in 2001, aged twenty-five, was the first great pivot I was able to make. From my life being all over the shop, from my head telling me I couldn't enjoy life if I didn't have a drink or a joint, to struggling through and going clean, to being able to actually enjoy my day-to-day and admit how I felt about snooker. To being where I am today.

I was ready for it. And because I was open to it, I met some fantastic people along the way.

You begin with the Twelve Steps, when you go through rehab. If you read each one as an outsider you might see a lot of God in there, or at least a lot of higher power. Well, you can take that where you want. A higher power can be anything that works for you. It can be an AA meeting or a Narcotics Anonymous meeting. It's anything that's more than one person. It's a power greater than you, on your own.

It's the good people you have around you. You can walk into a meeting feeling lost but come out feeling great from the collective power in the room. And it does lead to religion, for a lot of the ones you meet. I found the people who had the most palpable sense of inner peace were the ones who had found a Christian God, or Buddha. You could feel it coming off them in warm rays.

You also find people who come to the meetings who strike you as mad as hatters. And that's fine as well, because they're clean. They were also some of the most fun people to be around. There's a dark humour underpinning everything you do in rehab. You're all scraping along the bottom, so you're kind of liberated to take the piss out of everything, starting with yourself. You get flirty people in there. You get manipulation, of course, because not everyone is clean, and not everyone has worked out where they need to get to, and what they should probably stop doing. I was stumbling from one calamity to the next at times. I was chatting with another patient in one of my first meetings, and then became paranoid that I'd said something wrong, and that he thought I was a lunatic. I went as far as packing all my gear and getting a cab home, all the way across London from Roehampton to Chigwell. Four hours of feeling even worse, then a cab all the way back to be knocking on the clinic door again at midnight.

You get the hang of it, after a week or two. You start instinctively picking up the vibes. I could walk into a meeting and go, right, that's the sick corner, that's the get-well corner. You can tell by people's mannerisms – the way they sit, the way they are with themselves. One is fidgeting, he's getting his phone out and he's not looking over. He's still up to his neck in it all. Another bloke has got his cup of tea and is just listening, easy and calm. He's okay. He's making progress. Sit near him.

The dream scenario is that you go in and find yourself looking at someone thinking, I want what they've got. The first sponsor I was given looked like one of the calm ones, almost like he'd never been through anything too traumatic. Then he shared his story with the whole group, and it was . . . horrific.

There was heroin, there was crack. He came from a good family and had inherited a really good business, and none of it made any difference. It was like he was on a mission to destroy himself. He nearly died several times, and when you heard what he'd done, the only thing that surprised you was the nearly part. Then one day he got himself in a meeting somewhere, got into rehab, got clean and turned his life around.

You have to be truly living the Twelve Steps to be invited into the Priory. They wouldn't have let in one of what I used to call the nutty geezers, or what they refer to as the dry drunks – technically not on the sauce anymore, but in no way winning the battle. This bloke was the programme. You listened to him talking and thought, you were like that and now you're like this? He was bulletproof. That's how it seemed. He had his rules, his constants in place. He lived his new life and there was no deviating from it. I couldn't help but admire his attitude, even if I was miles away from that place myself. I was impressed by his willingness to go to such lengths to change.

The first step was blatantly clear to me. 'We admit we are powerless over our addiction and that our lives have become unmanageable.'

Step 2. 'We come to believe that a Power greater than ourselves could restore us to sanity.'

When I went to my first meeting I was in bits. This was the one that convinced me to go to rehab proper, to book into the Priory. I hated my life. I hated that I had become dependent on drugs. Then one guy in the group began speaking, and I became convinced someone had told him my story. Weed makes you paranoid, but this was really freaking me out. I was looking around the circle of chairs. Is there something going on here? It's a newbie thing, a rite of passage. I'm being tricked.

His story was my story. And he looked so happy and was so bubbly that it filled me with an unfamiliar hope. I came out of the meeting feeling fantastic, got home and celebrated in my usual way, which was rolling a nice fat spliff. That's how excited I was. *I am going into the Priory tomorrow, I might as well finish off this little bit I've got left.*

Clearly there were flaws in my thinking. But the meeting had become a power greater than me. It could restore me, when I started listening properly, and stopped thinking that the best way to get over your addiction to spliff was by smoking all the spliff you had in the house. From that point on, each meeting became a safe place for me. And that was quite an amazing feeling to have.

Step 3. 'We make a decision to turn our will and our lives over to the care of God.' Well, I really struggled with that one. I'm agnostic. God became the meetings. Steps two and three were interlinked for me.

Step 4. 'We make a searching and fearless moral inventory of ourselves.' Maybe that's sort of what I'm trying to do with this book. I never really made it past four in rehab, because that was like the advanced course. Had it been AA I went to, I would have rattled through all twelve in the space of four weeks, since they like to fast-track you. The book comes out and they get busy. Right, we've done one, two and three. You believe in this, that, right, you're on to the next one . . .

When I met my sponsor, it was a much deeper dive. A big folder, your working guide to the Twelve Step programme, 200 pages thick. Step 1 took us about two months. You're writing down heaps of stuff – the bad things you've done, the bad things you've loved doing, the way it makes you feel afterwards. My man's thinking was that unless you have a really sound step 1, you've always got the lurking doubt that you actually are an addict after all. Or, as he used to say, you're leaving the back door open. And I was leaving the back door open a lot of the time.

Later on, I got taken through the full twelve by someone I met who believed I needed it. He thought I needed all twelve or else I was done for. Back door, front door, all the ground-floor windows. His thing was trying to get me to accept that I was an addict, at a point when I couldn't accept it. I would say, How can I be? I am working, I am doing this and doing that. I've had a few joints and got a bit carried away, but you know, I'm not that bad, am I?

He got quite frustrated with me at times. He was such a believer in the programme that he couldn't see any other route to happiness for me. Almost like he was brainwashed. I saw him years later, maybe fifteen years down the line, and he was quite apologetic. Ron, I've changed as well, I was so militant it wasn't healthy. But at that moment I needed someone like him to help break the denial in me. He got me to the point where I truly accepted that I had an addictive personality.

I still think about him a great deal. Now, when I'm tempted to have a puff or pile into the Guinness, I can stop myself because I know where it's going to end up. Before I went through rehab, I would launch into the first spliff or pint and think, No worries, I can stop after the second or third one. But I never did. That was the thing. I'd stop two or three days later. It took the hard work I did with him, all the digging into my head and writing stuff down in those massive books, to accept I truly was an addict.

It was such a big moment for me. I kept dipping in and out until that point. I would get well, stay clean for three months or six months and then all of a sudden I would go on a mad bender. I'd love it, right up to the minute I absolutely hated it. All the alarm bells going off, the revulsion and the shame.

How the fuck have I ended up here? It's my daughter's birthday, and I am sitting here a total wreck in some random bloke's house . . .

Of all the steps, the one I probably spend most time with these days is number 10: 'We continue to take personal inventory and when we're wrong promptly admit it.'

For me that's about being aware of what I'm going through each day. I want to get the best out of myself. I don't like aimlessly doing stuff. I've become quite structured around my time. Asking myself if I'm pushing myself too hard, if I'm going to need a break, why I'm doing this, that and the other. It's putting a checklist in place, or maybe a safety net. You're continually looking at ways to tweak your life for the better. It's an optimisation.

I'm trying to stay in the game for as long as possible, trying not to burn myself out. Realising now that at forty-seven I have to be smarter than I ever have been before. I look at Rafa Nadal and Novak Djokovic. The reason they've enjoyed such long and fruitful careers was not just that they're extraordinarily good at what they do, but because they manage themselves. They're careful with their schedules, they say no to stuff. They look after their bodies; they look after their minds. They choose the right people to have around them and support them.

Step 11. 'We seek through prayer and meditation to improve our conscious contact with God as we understand Him, praying only for knowledge of His will for us and the power to carry that out.'

Well, I don't do prayer and I don't do meditation, but I am continually trying to stay in a good place. I run with Greg and Sonny, and I go to the caff with them afterwards for porridge. No prayer, but I try to surround myself with people who carry that kind of serene energy, that good vibe.

Step 12. 'Having had a spiritual awakening as the result of these steps, we try to carry this message to addicts and to practise these principles in all our affairs.'

That's okay for me, that one. The guy I mentioned who is sitting in a meeting and he's calm and relaxed – he's carrying a message for a newcomer who walks into the room. So is the fidgety one on his phone. It's just a different message. One that shows you the long and winding journey everyone has to go on.

Step 12 is about giving back. That's the way I interpret it in my life today. I do it through sport, through my running. Through talking about mental health.

All these things that have helped me, I try to be honest about them. When you've suffered with mental health issues you can empathise, and you can try to help others. I try to be authentic. I have had my struggles, and I find it fairly easy to open up about it, because I never was any good at lying.

I could never pretend to the world that everything is great. If you see me, I think, you can see right through me. And I thought the easiest way to deal with that was to say, yes, I am fucked sometimes, I am vulnerable, I do struggle.

All I've done is to try and fix some of those issues. Through the Twelve Steps, through running, through listening to good people who can teach you something. I always want to be open to it. When you go as low as I have, and come back as far, it becomes like a drug in itself. Feeling good, having your life in order, moving forward. It's not easy but you do it, and it's the best thing. Really, it is.

It doesn't have to be complicated, making your days good. We all think there's going to be one blinding revelation and suddenly it all comes good. Well, maybe that happens to you, and you're one of the lucky ones. But it's often the simple pleasures in life that help me tip the balance.

After I'd done those Twelve Steps, found that peace of mind within me, touched on a little spirituality, got myself clean, I found running. I'll talk about it more later, but it was like the second Twelve Steps for me. You've got the meeting, early in the morning in the woods or down at the track in the evening. You've got the fellowship with other runners. You're outside, you're producing natural endorphins for a natural high. You've got good people you want to spend time with. No one's there to talk about their jobs.

When you sprinkle each day with things you enjoy, the day becomes a good one. It might be you having a coffee with a friend. It might be taking your dog for a walk or giving yourself half an hour to read a book or make a meal you've never made before. It's never anything huge and obviously life-changing, but it adds up in the best kind of sneaky fashion. You can still get your work done and do all the ordinary tasks we all have to do, but you'll be more productive. You'll enjoy what you're doing. Incorporating small amounts of pleasure into every day makes me want to live. That's how powerful it can be.

Here's an example that would have shocked the party-boy Ronnie of old. At the World Championships, my favourite part of each day is that scone and clotted cream from Marks & Spencer. I'll have one every day, and it's a special moment every time. The cream and the sugar and the bread all sitting nice in my stomach.

Small things, big impacts. If I can stay in a good place mentally, I know I will perform better. I can't just switch it on and off; I have to establish a certain cadence to my life.

I've tried the chaos. I've lived at 100 miles an hour, I've been the manic man. Sometimes I'll still find myself doing it. I'll be at a tournament with a certain mate and he'll be all over the gaff – can't find his phone, can't find his keys. We're leaving at 2 p.m., except we're not now, we're leaving at 4 p.m., and I'm rushing to the venue and I can't pot a ball because I'm not settled.

It's not his fault. He's wonderful company, like a brother to me. He's stuck with me through everything. I just have to set boundaries. John, we'll have lunch at midday. I'm setting off at two, you come along when you want. I'll see you down there.

I'm terrible at going on holiday. I went ten years without one. I don't have the time, and I'm away so much with snooker that I don't want to see another hotel room. I want to be at home.

What I've tried to do is make my normal life more like a holiday. If I'm at a tournament, I'll get my run in. I'll have breakfast with those running friends. We might sit there chatting until one in the afternoon, ordering lunch, getting another coffee in. I might have to go to play some snooker at some point, but I've already had a great day.

You discover your own tricks and your own resilience. When I was going through my bad seven-year period from 1994, I didn't want to be sociable. I didn't feel good in my own skin. As I came out of rehab, I learned how to be in company without drugs and booze. I became a better listener than I had been. I worked out that when you're talking to someone you should truly listen to what they're saying, not just think about what you're going to say next.

You listen, and you learn. A little while ago I watched a documentary Tiger Woods did with Jada Pinkett Smith. She was telling him how inspirational he was, and he couldn't get it. He kept saying, I don't see it like that. I see everything as if it's a fight.

I get it. Your whole life at this level can become a tear up. You don't know how to do it any differently, and you're scared to let go. If I don't carry on being this person, then who am I?

You think, I am going to destroy everything and anyone who comes in my path, because that's where you feel in control. When you're winning and no one can touch you.

I was that way. I responded to every blow I felt. I saw every challenge life throws at you as a fight. Either I win or I'm finished.

But it doesn't have to be like that. It can't be. You can get away with it until a certain age, and then it becomes too exhausting. I've become aware of how much damage you do that way to yourself and others around you. You have to find a new way, a smarter way. That's all I've tried to learn.

Looking after your time makes a difference, in a sport like golf or snooker. You have to be in a calm place outside the game to flourish within it. It's not like working in an office, when you can have a bad day and go home and it's all done. In sport you have to get up each day and perform. You have to be better than the next guy coming at you. If you don't win at a tournament, you don't get paid. Each time you walk to the table you are playing for your livelihood.

Your life cannot be pandemonium. I've had to make it clear to people around me that they won't always get an instant reply from me. It might be three or four days until a text gets answered. Don't bombard me with questions and dates and fancy a bit of this, Ronnie? It will get done when the balance in my life allows.

I felt trapped when I thought like snooker was all I had. It was taking so much from me, and it was unhealthy, but I couldn't do without it.

When I found other parts of my day that didn't involve as much emotion, it helped my head and it fed back into my playing too. That became my job. Snooker was a hobby. And as soon as snooker became something I was choosing to do, everything became a bonus. If I had a win, great. If I didn't, I had other things to look forward to.

I don't want that old life anymore. I don't want to be involved. You may well have been through a similar arc in your own career; throwing yourself into your job, sacrificing your private time for the next gig or the next promotion, pulling early starts and late nights and doing extras at the weekend, not just because they want you to but because you think you should, because you think it's all going to pay off in some way. Instead you become a tight little ball of stress, and it leaks out in other ways – arguments at home, drinking too much, lying awake at night unable to sleep. Snooker is no different. It drives you to where the dark stuff manifests.

I have had to navigate my way out of it. And once it becomes a quest for you, staying in the good place, you stay open to all sorts of stuff you might have shut off in the past. In China, pre-Covid, I got into a conversation about the ageing process. I found out about this idea, in Chinese culture, that you have two lives: your birth to the age of forty, and then forty to whenever it might end. You change as a person in the middle of your life – what you want to do, what you need.

It struck a chord with how I had been feeling. It's about controlling the pace, as you get older. Embrace where you are. Your joy comes from continuing to do what you love, but to do it well, you need the time and space to dedicate yourself to it, and the time and space to be free of it too.

Damien Hirst has been telling me the same thing. Ronnie, you're a snooker player, I'm an artist. People want stuff from us all the time. They lob deadlines at us. We have to control the pace, or we will lose the happiness that doing our thing brings. He calls it driving the car in whatever direction you want to drive it. You're behind the wheel. It's up to you where you want to go. So now I listen to my gut instinct, when something comes along. Does this feel right or not? It's why I took a year out from snooker after winning the world title in 2012. I barely made a tournament. That for me was about controlling the pace, not chasing things, keeping my life in a good place.

So this is me, today, back in front of the mirror. Looking at me looking back at myself.

I know I want to play snooker. I know too that I can't go too deep in, because the moment I do that all my triggers are set off. Then we go through the whole cycle – getting my mind back, getting my health back, getting the anxiety under control, and off we go again.

The penny dropped when I went to rehab. I was playing snooker like a machine, and I hit rock-bottom and I didn't realise why I was down there. Only when they said to me, it's an inside job. Inside job, how? Ronnie, you've got to start feeling good about yourself on the inside.

And they were right. The things that are really important in life come free most of the time. You don't have to pay for peace of mind and serenity. You just have to find whatever it is that creates it for you.

I started to realise that it's not what I spend, it's not what car I drive, it's not where I live. It's about being comfortable in my own skin, and I think that will never leave me. I realised that no matter what situation I am in, being fit and being healthy is so important. Walking the mountains, taking time out, reading, switching the phone off. The food I put in my body. All of these things have become really important to me.

Going for a run on a cold morning, getting in and having a cup of tea and a scone? That's brilliant, to me. Borrowing a mountain bike and going out into the Peak District? A great morning. I know most people might think I'm mad. The people I like hanging out with don't. It's my world and it's their world.

Remember the dimmer switch. The light is never off. You just play around with the brightness.

7

PRACTICE
HAPPY PLACE

In the front door, left into the lounge, through the kitchen with its white units, past the utility room on the right. That's how you get to the snooker room at my mum's house.

It's a bit cold in here, slightly damp. An October evening, leaves hanging off the trees. Dew settling on the grass of pavement verges and front gardens. Misty in the quiet suburban streets.

Pale walls, beige carpet, brown curtains across the window and the patio doors. Small table in the corner by the single upright chair. The lovely bright green of the table, lit by the light hanging above, dark wood frame, lighter brown leather round the pockets.

I love it in here. This is where I find my meditative state. This is the calm time.

Sometimes my favourite hour to come is ten o'clock at night. It feels like everyone else is asleep and I've got the whole universe to myself. I can turn my phone off. Sit down there on the chair, stick my ashtray and fags on the table. Next time I look up it's midnight, and that's such a buzz for me, the way time compresses. I sleep well after those nights.

It's a happy place, this snooker room. It's not been decorated for a while; the table is a little heavy and slow from the dampness in the air. If you want a drink or food you have to go back into the kitchen and see what leftovers Mum's stashed away in various little plastic containers in her fridge. She can never throw away food, Mum. Goes back to when her and Dad were growing up, and she was cooking for most of her family too, and you never wasted anything.

It doesn't matter how it looks. In here I'm in control of what I'm doing. No one else is coming in to mess things up and get in my head. It's all simple, in here.

The table, the balls, my cue. No distractions, no noise, no expectations.

So I set up the balls in a line between the centre pockets. Maybe fifteen or sixteen of them, mix of reds and colours, doesn't make any difference. You just need the numbers. You don't want to be walking round the table loads of times. It interrupts the practice, the groove you're looking for.

I leave the white up by the baulk line, and I take them on one by one, a mid-range long pot into the far corner pockets.

I should be making them from here, but it's more about the ball-striking. That's what we're working on: my potting stance, how my hips feel, my arm. Where the bridge hand is, how low to the table I'm getting. If I miss the pot, that can be okay. I watch where the white ball goes afterwards, and that gives me a guide. If it's behaving itself, we can still be all good.

All of us have things to work on, the top players. My tendency is to get too steep with my cue, when I want it to be closer to parallel with the table. This drill is about getting my trajectory right. When I'm good, when I'm cueing as I'd like, I can wing it with the shots I go for. I've got more to play with.

I wonder, sometimes, when I'm sitting down with a fag, thinking about it all. I'm not sure it would feel as good in here if I hadn't struggled with my game for so long. Because I had such a prolonged period of self-doubt, I'm much more grateful to be here with it all working – or rather, being able to fix it, when it's going wrong.

Let's try a red to the corner. Okay, it's gone in, but there's no pleasure in that one for me. My hips weren't great, my bridge wasn't quite right.

Next ball in the line. Chalk out of my right trouser pocket, one dab on my cue tip, slip it back into my pocket.

Miss it. Miss the next one, by even more.

Years ago, I would have been panicking at this point. When you're not striking the cue ball well, the area of the pocket you can hit begins to shrink. What I'm trying to do is get the butt of the cue going through the middle of the white, the middle of the red, right to the wide part of the pocket. So we'll attempt another one.

Butt of the cue feels good. Pull it back, pause . . . through the ball.

That was a better one. I can work with that. A positive strike, powerful, hitting through the line. The pause at the end of your backswing gives you time. You don't pull the cue back and just go BANG. It gives you no feel, no compression on the white. The pause slows you down, and when you're playing well, you feel like you can hold it that bit longer, but it's not an easy thing to do. Everyone's pull-back is their own. It's where you can be robotic or full of flare.

That's a good strike. Proper good.

You watch the white as much as where the object ball has ended up. A bad shot is if the white slides across the table after impact, because it means I'm cutting across it.

Bad miss, that one. The red hit the far knuckle of the pocket. This is when you start to doubt yourself.

Everything has to be pushed towards the line you want to pot – your arms, your body, your knees. Your weight must be balanced. Then the cue just sits on your body, tucked in, as much a part of you as your arm or your head.

Here's another secret for you. You pot from your hips. The more you're leaning into the table, working with the table, the more you can get effort and power and accuracy with your cueing action. It's like downforce on a car, making it grip through corners more. Get the hips right, and you're solid and in control. If I start messing up a few pots, I work on my body.

Miss.

I can live with that one. Hips felt good, I'm starting to fancy it.

Chalk cue, get down.

Good pot.

When you're tweaking little things in your game, it takes a while to calibrate it all. When it's starting to come, you know. You can feel it.

I played Barry Hawkins in a practice match a few days before this. Turned into a right heavy day, because I couldn't get my arm right. I had to make shifts, try subtly different set-ups and approaches. Oh, the nightmares I've had down the years, when the magic was there, and then suddenly not there, and I had to find it again! It took me four frames against Hawkins to get it right, but it was all good, because I was able to turn it around, and Hawkins is a top player. It was proper fun and games.

My last shot was what I call a good bad shot. I missed it, but my hips were in the right place, so I got away with my arm not being great. If your hips aren't in the right place, nothing else matters. Great arm, perfect bridging hand, bad hips . . . you're done for.

It's starting to come now . . .

With it comes the buzz, the rush of pleasure. I feel like I've just figured it out in two shots. You don't want to be doing this two days before the Masters or the UK Championships; you want to trust in what you're doing at that point. But the desire to have this feeling is always with you. After the World Championships in 2022, I left Sheffield thinking, that was good, but can I do better?

That last shot felt good. Oh mate! Suddenly I feel like I'm playing on a pool table. Everything's shrunk . . .

I feel like everything's pushing down into the floor. I feel strong.

I could walk away now, it's that good. But then walking away . . . you hear the stories of players who didn't put the hours in, and it always catches up with them. There's track athletes out there who will run one hard lap of the track and feel great and not bother doing anything else that day. I'd rather do the Cristiano Ronaldo method and put in two hours extra. Make sure. Don't give it the chance to slip away from you.

It's about time management, when you want to be the best. It's about optimisation.

You have to make sure you build in rest days, you have to make sure you don't burn out. Time is our most important asset, whether you're playing snooker or trying to make your life work. I keep a diary of all this: all the practice sessions I do, how I feel about them. A note in my phone, with the days I've practised and how long I've gone for. Emojis next to each entry to remind me how I felt. A smiley face for a good day, teeth gritted face for a frustrating day. It helps keep you steady. It keeps you doing the good stuff.

I started this block of practice about four weeks ago. The first week I came here three days and played for three hours each time. The other days I ran, and went to the gym, and did my Pilates.

Each week it builds. Ten hours the following week, twelve the next. When you go beyond the three/four-hour point in one session you start to dip in and out. You get tired and start to lose your game. But you also need to build up your tolerance to become battle-hardened.

The notes in my phone tell me when the adaptations will come. A fourteen-hour week, a sixteen-hour week. Twenty hours, and there's no point in playing a tournament. You're too tired. You're spending these hours on this table to win the tournament in three weeks' time.

I've got my trust in data because I don't trust myself. I can't trust myself. There's no point; my emotions get in the way, and when I get too emotional, I'm all over the place. I have to write things down and become scientific – a sleep diary, a running diary, a snooker diary. That way it's all written down, it's all done.

Maybe it's something you do already. If not, I recommend it. It takes no time, it's easy, and it's free. What has made you happy that day? What went well, and what would you change?

When I make my notes, I put that to bed. I've done everything that I know is right for me. Now I have to hand it over to the snooker gods and let everything come together.

No one taught me how to play when I was a kid. It was all feel, all instinct. It was wonderful while it lasted, but I didn't understand how it worked. It just happened. That's why before, when I was struggling, if I suddenly started cueing well, I'd put my cue away and go home. I was terrified of breaking the spell.

Now I'll carry on playing, because I'm confident it will all be there the next day, and if it isn't, I can put it right.

Down into my stance again. This is feeling tight and compact. My arm feels terrible, but because I'm compact, I can hold it all strong and together, and I feel as if I have all the time in the world. Lovely. If I didn't feel compact, and I didn't feel like I had the time, and I still potted it, there'd be no satisfaction and no happiness. It wouldn't matter. I'd know.

My hips were good there. My hips were strong, proper strong. I don't care I missed the pot, the ball rattling in the jaws. Hips felt great. About an eight out of ten for that. About an eight.

I could do this for hours, honestly, I could. This is pure meditation for me, as beautiful and pure as anything in my world. That's why I can't give it up. There's nothing in the world I can get this buzz from.

I watch the old videos of me playing, and I always see something I'd like to improve. I watch them and I can't believe how far away from my body my bridge hand is, and it's like looking at a famous old painting and suddenly spotting a flaw in the depiction of one character. A lot of the time you're potting from the position of that front hand. When you get it right it doesn't matter so much what your back hand is doing. You feel you could stand on one leg and pot balls if your front hand is right.

But you can't keep thinking technique. You lose yourself in it, in the end. I do.

It's *feel* that matters in the big matches. How quickly can I get down to this pot? How comfortable can I get doing it? When I'm bang on it, I get in that position fast, and that's the mental place where I have to be, where every elite sports person has to be. You can't be thinking: cue down, hips here, my arm's not right, hand forward, I'm feathering it too much . . . On the practice table here, it might work. Out there, under pressure, it doesn't happen. I've been there too many times, and it's scary. Your world falls apart around you.

Hips felt strong there. Good pot. Hips feel strong on this one too. Another pot.

I wonder, on quiet late nights like this: when I retire, will this room, will any practice table, still feel like a place of calm to me? That worry is almost one of the reasons why I don't want to retire. Why I want to keep playing and keep enjoying it. I think I saw it in Roger Federer in his last few years before he quit. He still loved the game, and he still loved the feeling of being able to play amazing shots. It's just his body wouldn't allow him to do it to that level anymore, yet he won't get that feeling any other way. That's what haunts you.

So I'm enjoying this. I'm appreciating what it's doing for me. I might have my moan-ups, but as long as I still fancy it, and I'm getting my kicks from it, I try to plot a path to the day I can't play at the competitive level I want. Forty-seven years old now, and you can see it in the distance: when I'm doing exhibitions rather than world finals.

I can convince myself I'll be okay with getting beaten. What I won't be okay with is if I'm not playing well, and people have come to see me, and I'm losing the crowd. If they're happy to see a testimonial, if it's about saying you've seen me, not the player making 147s in five minutes but nice 80s and 90s and shots you want to tell your mates about afterwards – that's all okay. It's like the Rolling Stones. No one goes to see them in concert to hear new material or a new version of an old song. They just want to say they've seen the Stones. They want to hear a version of 'Satisfaction' or 'Sympathy for the Devil' that sounds like the records.

Not every old player manages it. With Stephen Hendry it

was all about the winning. When he wasn't winning, the game wasn't enough for him. Steve Davis was all about winning too, but then he discovered he could find enjoyment from simply playing. I can imagine him practising like I am now, hitting a few long pots, feeling good, thinking, *That was nice.* There were times towards the end of his career when he looked like he was on holiday. That's where you want to be. All the pressure gone, just appreciating it for its own sake, in that moment.

And enjoyment is the key to it all, if you're going to sustain it. When I watched Usain Bolt in the Olympic finals he looked like he was loving every minute of it. That was his superpower, and that's the ultimate, for all of us at the top of our games, the place where everyone wants to be. Bolt had the ability, as soon as he settled into his blocks, to switch on. Steve Peters told me to do the same. Ten minutes before you play, switch on.

These pots I'm taking on now are about fancying it. The same drill, balls out of the pockets and back in a long cramped line from centre pocket to centre pocket, white up by the baulk. If I fancy it, it goes in, and when I'm moving into position for the next one, I've got that bounce in my step.

Oh, that's a bad miss . . . It made a horrible sound. Absolutely horrible. I felt a bit inside on the white, too over the top of the ball, not behind it enough. And it's too late to adjust, when you're down in your stance. It's not worth getting up and settling again, because all of a sudden you're doing it all the time.

Another miss.

Another terrible feeling. See, this is where panic can set in. It won't, but it can.

Another miss.

It feels like I'm slapping the ball now. If that had gone in, I still wouldn't have cared. I'd rather miss it than pot a bad one.

That one felt decent. This one . . . not bad.

Micro-adjustments all the time, and you can lose yourself in them. The problem is you can never quite see yourself as you are. I realised that when I read Joe Davis's book, *How I Play Snooker*. It might have first come out in 1949, but there is so much wisdom in there, and one of the big lessons was that you need someone else to watch you too. I know it's a bit mad, taking inspiration from a book older than my dad. It's like Tiger Woods leaning on the technical teachings of Sam Snead or Ben Hogan. But it chimed for me.

We don't often have the ability to assess ourselves properly. I remember beating Barry Hawkins in the final of the 2016 Masters, and I was convinced I'd played terrible. Hadn't deserved it at all. I asked a friend who was watching what they thought. They said I'd been brilliant. I ignored it, because I thought I knew better.

About five years later, I was messing about on YouTube, and I came across the match highlights. I didn't want to watch, because I thought it would depress me. Rubbish snooker getting a lucky result. But I watched anyway, and I was astonished. I was playing really well – lovely snooker. It was like watching a different player in another tournament. The weirdest thing of all? I won that match 10-1. The biggest winning margin in a final of my entire career. How mad is that?

There is such a strong lesson for us in that story, in the obsession with everything being absolutely flawless. Sometimes you have to ignore your feelings of doubt. Stop asking yourself if you're doing something right or wrong, and just get on with it. Put one foot in front of the other. Do what you set out to do.

It's so easy to criticise ourselves. Someone's doing this better than me. I'm not doing it well enough. I'm not even doing it like I was yesterday. Maybe you're in the gym and you're feeling slow and tired. Maybe you're cooking a meal, and it looks nothing like the photos in the recipe book. You're in a meeting at work and you can't get your words out.

Sometimes you just have to keep doing it. Lighten the weight and finish your reps, serve the meal messy but tasty, make your point. Get over the first hurdle and move on to the next one. It doesn't mean we don't strive for perfection, but it can't be at the detriment of being happy and actually getting the job done. Find that meditative state where you focus on being content with doing the best you can. And listen to feedback from people you trust. Sometimes they're able to see things you miss in yourself.

Anyway, it's starting to get cold in here now. Coming up to midnight, Mum in bed hours ago. No noise from the road at the front of the house, everyone tucked up. Three outside walls to this room, and you can touch the slight clamminess on the paint, feel the cloth on the table slowing up a little. Not great for positional play, not when the tournament tables will be quicker.

You have to get low over your shots. That's another secret.

It shortens the distance between the white and the object ball. If you do it properly it feels like the white is on top of the red. The red, the white and the cue are all in a straight line. It makes the game so much easier. If I'm a bit steep over the white, I'm having to look up slightly to the red, and a little thing like that can stop you playing well.

Good pot. Good feeling.

The power you can put through the white? That comes from timing. There's players on the circuit with unbelievable timing and power, and it all flows from their set-up. If you get that right, it allows you to really thrash through the ball. No one has ever hit the ball like Neil Robertson, and his power means I have to be at 100 per cent for 90 per cent of the match to be sure I'm going to beat him. If I'm 100 per cent for 80 per cent I might still get past him, but if I drop down to 70 per cent, I'll lose. I believe his good game isn't as good as my good game, but he's more consistent, so it's a good match-up. I might beat him 10-7, 10-8, but I'm never going to blow him away.

Then there's other players who you see fighting their cue, and they have to tone down the power to keep accuracy. Men like Ken Doherty, James Wattana and maybe Mark Allen. In some ways it limits them, but they always make up for it in other areas, become very good tactically. When a frame goes scrappy they're comfortable, because they play a lot more like that. You don't really want to be up against players who can do that. I'd rather be playing someone more natural, because you can feed off it.

Time to work on my right to left pots. These are more of an issue for me, these days. When I was a kid, it was fine, but since I had my problems, this side has been a struggle.

Good strike.

Solid set-up, plenty of time with the pull. I can hold, hold, hold . . . then let it go.

Now this cue feels so short in my hand. Lovely. I'm really giving it some welly, but it's accurate too. My left hip has become the guide. I'm on it.

When I was a kid, it happened all the time. Then I lost it for seven years. The game became difficult, and I didn't remember it being difficult. That's why I struggled mentally with it.

Even after all these years it's astonishing how small an adjustment can make such an instant and significant difference. Maybe that's why this sport does your nut in. I was 3-1 down to Ricky Walden at the Welsh Open early in 2022, and it wasn't happening for me. Then I moved the middle finger on my bridging hand maybe five millimetres further towards my first finger, and it all began to change. My bridging hand is my left, when I'm playing normally – the one that provides the groove for the front of the cue to glide through. (You pot from your front hand, when you're playing well. Steve Davis used to have a beautiful bridge hand – you can probably picture it in your head.)

The middle finger almost immediately became the guide line for my eye to follow, like the sight on a rifle. And that little tweak transformed my play. I made breaks of 88 and 85, and thought, if I win this match, I'm going to win the tournament.

Sod's law, the snooker gods looked down at me and said, You're not having this match, Ronnie, not this time. Ricky played a great safety shot in the deciding frame, got in and knocked off 83, and saw me off. But from that match onwards, that middle finger got me fancying the job. That middle finger won me the World Championships two months later. Something as inconsequential as that.

When you find that little bit of form, it transforms you. Everything about you.

Before the Worlds in 2016 I was in a mess. I beat Dave Gilbert 10-7 in the first round, and afterwards I felt utterly overwhelmed by how far away I was from where I thought I should be, by how maddening this sport was. I smashed my cue in the dressing room, rammed the butt into the wall. I couldn't speak to anyone – not the press, not the TV people. World Snooker gave me a formal warning. You can't behave like this. Not here.

What they didn't know was that I'd had a complete breakdown. I left the Crucible and drove all the way back to London, straight to the Nightingale Hospital in Marylebone. 'I can't take this anymore.' That was all I could say to the doctor. 'I need a rest.'

They gave me some tablets. Lorazepam, like a Valium. A benzodiazepine, designed to treat anxiety.

I didn't want to take the pills at first. I stayed in there on the Monday night, the Tuesday night, the Wednesday. I still wasn't well enough to even think about playing snooker. So I relented, and swallowed my medicine, and within half an hour I was flying. A new man.

I went back to Sheffield. Picked up my cue from the menders, glad it was the butt I'd smashed, because you can fix that, and walked out for my second-round match against Barry Hawkins.

I wasn't a new man. I was the same man and the same player, but the fear had gone, the mad panic. Racking up the breaks, piling up the points. I made 10 breaks over 70, four centuries, scored almost a quarter as many points again as he did. Trouble was, I'd played so many exhibitions that year and so few tournaments that I was a fraction loose in the tight frames. 7-4 down, 10-8 down, 12-9 down, and I got it back to 12-12 and a decider. If we'd been 6-6 I would have had him, except the match had gone so deep he fancied the job. I'd left it too late. But I'd rediscovered the magic. His first win over me in a competitive match for fourteen years, only the second time in thirteen years I hadn't made the quarter-finals at the Crucible. Yet I knew if I'd won that match, I would have fancied winning the tournament.

Back to the here and now. Back to this table, late at night, in a quiet suburb full of sleeping people.

I lose time, here. That's nice, when you've had insomnia like me, when you're scared of spending too much time in your own head.

I don't want to lose the form I had at the 2022 Worlds, I think. Then I think back further, to the World Championship in 2012, and I remember how good I felt then.

RIGHT It was all natural, when I was a kid. All feel. No one ever coached me. I could just see balls, and pot balls.

LEFT No wonder my mum looks excited. It's actual Alex Higgins. Some people wanted me to be his wild man successor, but while I loved the way he played the game, I could never live the same life.

ABOVE It takes something special to succeed at the Crucible, and it's not always the ones you expect. Joe Johnson was my first Sheffield crush.

LEFT I loved obsessing over the tiny nuances of the game. And I reckon my technique, when I was about 14, was as good as it has ever been since.

RIGHT Bit of a chunky monkey in this one. I always loved my food. But like a lot of things in my life, it took me a long time to work out how to say no.

LEFT The world around you changes, when you win big at 17. Suddenly everybody wants to be your mate. Suddenly everyone wants a slice.

RIGHT Five minutes for a 147? I was out of control, but sometimes you can get away with out of control for a while. It's weird watching that frame back now. Like looking at someone I only half recognise.

RIGHT I learned so much from Stephen Hendry – not least when he beat me in big matches, like the semis at the Worlds in 1999. He's still an absolute hero to me. He was a machine, in the best possible sense.

LEFT Coming good in the World final of 2001, finding a way past John Higgins. And that's always a massive battle. I nearly blew it at the end, too.

RIGHT Uh-oh. What about this picture looks good to you? Exactly. I find it hard to take these sorts of images in. An unhappy kid, making everything much worse for himself.

LEFT That first world title was like a massive weight coming off my shoulders. I should have won one earlier. I was starting to think I never would.

LEFT I started running and everything immediately started to change. Don't worry about the shorts – they make sense when you're a runner.

RIGHT Cheeky cuppa before my morning run. That's how I manage to get out of bed so early, even when I'm tired and sore – just think about getting the kettle on. All the good stuff follows from there.

LEFT I love taking Osho for his walks. I love coming home to him too. Best part of the day.

RIGHT Time for a bit of dot painting with Damien Hirst. He loves his snooker, Damien, and gets the person I am. I've learnt loads from him. My painting's getting there too.

LEFT World quarter-final against Neil Robertson in 2012. One of my best-ever wins. Robertson's an incredible potter. Coming up against him drags the best out of you.

RIGHT Keeping Ali Carter in his seat in the final in 2012. I'd been working with Steve Peters for a year; my head felt great and my body followed suit.

LEFT Imagine how it feels to have your boy with you when you do something you always dreamed of doing. He's like a little surfer dude, Ronnie Junior. Nothing seems to bother him.

ABOVE Of all my friends in snooker, it's Jimmy White I'm maybe closest to. Jimmy's highs and lows are maybe higher and lower than anyone else to have ever played the game. It makes sense why we get on.

LEFT My mate Stoney, who we lost to cancer in the past year. You never got to know him, but I did, and I miss him all the time.

RIGHT The Hong Kong Masters in autumn 2022, and a world record crowd for a big snooker final. I went into it miserable, and came out of it reborn.

ABOVE Me and Laila. She's been a constant source of support and love to me down the years.

RIGHT Preparing for battle, backstage before another big final. You want no one near you in these lonely moments. Just you, your plotting and your dreams.

ABOVE Ronnie Junior all grown up, with his sister Lily after I won my seventh world title. I can't tell you how happy it made me having the two of them there. Actually, I can: it was absolutely amazing.

LEFT When it all seems worth it. When all the doubts and self-sabotage slip away. When I'm back playing pure snooker, for the pure love of a beautiful game.

It was frightening, the snooker I was coming out with. I couldn't believe how well I was hitting the ball. I had every shot in the world. After working with Steve Peters for a year, my head was good, too. Until 2011 I'd been playing well for one week and then shit for six. With Steve it was six weeks shit and two good, then three good, three poor, then four and five good. Consistency instead of the old frustration. Lovely.

So now the games begin in my head again. Maybe I should go back to my 2012 set-up. As soon as that thought's come along, the next one enters my brain: You know what, that could go tits up – maybe I should stick with what I've got, because this feels alright. It's working okay, standing and setting up in the correct place by the table to perceive the potting angle better; chalking my cue, popping it into my right pocket, down into my stance, everything tucked in, tight down the line.

Stay in the moment, Ronnie. This is the happy place. Breathe, and let it happen.

Another pot. Another one that feels good. That has that fatter sound.

Thunk.

I'm floating the pots in now. That's an amazing sign. That's ultimate control. A lot of people want to thrash at it, to punch it in. When you're really confident, you can feel your way through the flow instead.

I'm more scientific in my approach than I used to be. But I still don't really understand why it's all happening. I'm still about feel, deep down.

But I'll keep working at it. Keep coming to this cold room, this quiet place. Because I can hear it, in here. I can play with the sound.

Just me, and the balls, and the table.

8

FAMILY
AIN'T HE LOUD?

Here's a scene frozen in time for you. We're in Sheffield for the World Championships. It's 2022, post Covid, big crowds in. An evening session, so everyone's piling in through the foyer, grabbing their drinks, hurrying through to their seats.

It's quiet outside now. Barely anyone on Tudor Square, the spring light in the sky fading, streetlights coming on.

Just one bloke, in his late sixties. Black waterproof coat on, dark blue woolly hat. Grey goatee, trimmed short.

He's pacing up and down. From the front door of the theatre all the way out to Surrey Street, then turning on his heels and coming back past the Sheffield Library Theatre. Loop after loop, staring at his phone, shouting every now and then. Ignoring the few other people walking past, although there's something about his manner that says he doesn't want interrupting. Whatever he's lost in seems to make him simultaneously very happy and extremely stressed.

This is my dad. Ronnie O'Sullivan senior. Big Ron.

He'll get to watch my match later. He's recorded it, and when he gets back to the hotel, he'll watch the bits when I'm at the table, pause it when my opponent comes in, make himself a cup of tea and then forward until they're done at the table and then watch me again.

But I won't let him in the venue, not until the match is done. It's too much for me. I remember when I was a kid, eight years old and nine, and his presence at a competition used to put so much pressure on me. If I missed a shot I could hear his response – 'You're throwing it away . . .'

He loved watching me practise. Him and his mates in the snooker club, him holding court as always but almost never taking his eyes off me. He'd talk to me afterwards like I was a boxer, like his uncles had been. 'Take his fucking head off, son!'

The nerves would kill me. Over a shot thinking, I don't want to miss this, because Dad will get the hump. By the age of twelve we'd worked it out. When I'm playing, you go elsewhere. And it worked, because when I was twelve, I started winning everything. I knew it then. You're not good for me, in here.

He was good when I got home in the evening. He was good to talk to about the match and how it had been. But when it came to playing, I didn't need him there. So I told him again, in the last few years of his prison sentence: when you come out, you can come to the venue but not be in the crowd. I don't want to see you, don't want to feel you. I can feel your energy. You want me to win so bad it almost makes you angry, and I don't want to win that bad. I like the game, I think about what I do, and I want to enjoy it. If I win, great. If I don't, I ain't that bothered so long as I've enjoyed it. Alright?

He was always this way. Like Tiger Woods's father, Earl. All about winning. And I get it, because if you've grown up in poverty and there's something that'll mean you could swap that poverty for something else, why wouldn't you do it? Doesn't matter if it was a long time ago in your life. When you come from nothing all you think about is getting out of the gutter, and you never lose that mentality. Me? I never had to develop that mentality. My mum and dad did well as adults, and my childhood was an easy ride. I wanted to make the most of the opportunity my love for snooker gave me, but not like he did. Not like he still does.

He was always strict with me, all the way up to the moment I first fought back. It was a year or so before he went away, me sixteen years old, him dishing out the usual bollocking – you're not dedicating yourself, you need to get out running, you need to cut back on them burgers.

This time, I stood up to him. Shrugged my shoulders, told him I was packing my bags. Told them I was going to live and play in Scotland, sign a contract with Stephen Hendry's manager Ian Doyle, which Doyle had been badgering me to do for ages anyway.

I'll never forget the way they looked at me, my mum and dad. The first time they didn't tell me to go to my room, the first time they didn't raise the stakes and get into a right old shouting match. You could see it on their faces: he's sixteen years old now, he shaves like a man, he plays snooker like a man. And I could feel it inside me: as long as I've got my cue, no one can control me anymore. Me and my cue, we will be alright no matter where we go in the world. Like I was the character Rod Stewart's singing about in 'Maggie May'.

I didn't have a clue. I was still sixteen years old when he went to prison in 1992, jailed for the murder of a man called Bruce Bryan. An argument over a bar bill in some club in Chelsea, weapons pulled, weapons used.

I was away at a tournament in Thailand when it all happened. Crying my eyes out in some lonely hotel corridor, battering my cue against the walls. Flying home wide awake and in a daze at the same time.

They took me straight to Brixton prison when I got home. The mad incongruity of me being in a stretch limo, because my manager Barry Hearn had laid one on to pick me up from Heathrow, and pulling up outside this grey Victorian prison with its high brick walls and security cameras swooping and flashing and tall chimneys. Already seeing a change in Dad, in the look in his eyes and the leanness in his cheeks. No flashy gear anymore, just the same old clothes as everyone else, the same hollow look.

He was out on bail for a while, awaiting his court case at the Old Bailey, and I could sort of compartmentalise it then. Everything always worked out with my dad. Everyone told me it was going to work out again, right up to the point when the jury found him guilty and the judge gave him a twenty-year sentence.

I felt like I'd lost my spine when he went. My coach, my driving force; my idol, really. There was no chance he might be out in five or six years with good behaviour. Twenty years was going to be twenty years. The sums were straightforward. When he comes out again, I'll be thirty-six years old. My career will be over. I'm fucked, aren't I?

At fifteen years old I felt like the complete player. Everything was geared towards success. I was going to be Tiger, I was going to be Mike Tyson. Then all of a sudden, overnight, it fell apart, and I was lost and utterly bewildered. How am I going to get through this?

I'd go to tournaments and see other players there with their families, getting on, going out for tea, looking after each other. Safe little units. I didn't have any of that now. I didn't fit in anymore. It was horrendous. I had no idea how to behave. So obviously I went off the rails instead.

He was allowed three visits a month, in the first few years. I was travelling to tournaments around the country and beyond, but I'd always go to see him in Wormwood Scrubs over in White City at least once a month. You couldn't take him food or presents; other people had been caught stuffing things in cakes and teddy bears, so that was out.

I'd turn up each time thinking it was my job to cheer him up, to tell him a few jokes. On his own all day and night in a cell, no mates, worrying about his wife and son and daughter on the outside. Instead, he was always the one cheering me up.

There were a couple of moments when we had a cry together. The rest of the time he would be trying to make me laugh, or taking the piss out of the other people we could both see. He's a weird character, like that. Not your normal man. Neither did he seem to have a resentful bone in his body. Things happen when you're in prison – on the inside, where you're stuck, and on the outside, where you can't do anything. I'd be the angry one now, watching people he'd trusted screw him over while he couldn't touch them. Me fuming to him – you've given this geezer the shirt off your back, always helped him and his family, and now he's ripping you off. Him shrugging and trying to calm me down. Don't matter, Ronnie. Don't worry about it.

I don't think he was trying to protect me. He never did when I was little. Most of the other kids at primary school walked in with their mum or dad. He always sent me on my own. When I asked him why, he told me he wanted me to learn to cope with being on my own, because when I was sixteen or seventeen it might be that way.

He can't have known. Not really. But then I really was sixteen, and I had no choice but to be on my own, and maybe I was better prepared for it as a result. Maybe it was a blessing in disguise. A kid pretending to be a man even when he still felt like a kid inside.

It's a long slow grind when you're inside. It took three years of his sentence before he had access to a telephone. When he did, he would phone me every day. Talk about snooker, of course. He always wanted to know about the snooker. Give me a rocket or two up the arse. You on the practice table, Ronnie? You get a run in this morning? Not up late again, were you?

A few years further on, he was allowed access to a television. That really was a game-changer. Now he could watch me playing in the big tournaments, and you could see the difference it made to him. He would say to me, seeing you play is like having you in for a visit.

Difference to him? It changed me too. If there was no other reason to keep playing, it was enough that it was helping to keep my dad going. All the motivation I needed.

I used to watch Tiger Woods in his younger years. The first person he hugged after every major win, after his caddy, was his dad. It was like he was doing it for Earl as much as for himself. And that was the same as me, when Dad was away. I couldn't put my cue down in victory and hug him. But I could picture him in front of his little square TV in his cell, jumping around and whooping, shouting to all his mates on the wing that his boy had done it again.

They build the visits up slowly. You get to the point where you're allowed a couple of hours. And I'd be baffled by how he'd be laughing all the time. You'd hear stories from other prisoners who'd got to know him, not that you ever have much of an option with my dad.

'Ronnie, we love your old man, he keeps everyone going. Ain't he loud?'

'Ronnie, when he's not on the wing it's so dull. When they moved him off, we thought, fucking brilliant, we'll have a bit of peace and quiet now. Then after a couple of weeks, we were all saying, you know what, we fucking miss him . . .'

'Ronnie, can you get your dad back on our wing, yeah?'

Those conversations made me happier than anything.

My dad is going to be alright in here . . .

When people are in prison they have nothing. Material things lose their meaning. What matters is connecting – the bonds you can form with other humans, the relationships you can make and maintain. Dad's gift was to make people laugh, make them feel happy, and so he was genuinely liked. He kept an eye out for people. A lot of the inmates he knew in there would do things – run schemes, chance their arm, get in trouble. He'd be in their ear.

'Listen, don't do that. Give me that, I'll get rid of it, otherwise you're done for.'

He's a logical man. He's not impulsive. He planned it out.

I ain't going to be bitter, this ain't twisting me.

But he was in there, and I was out here, and I needed other people to lean on in his absence. To put me back on the rails when I flew off them.

My best mate as a kid was George Palacaros. We went to primary school together, we went to secondary school together. We pretty much used to live together. I would have his bed, he would stick a mattress on the floor. His mum Lula used to cook for us every day. She was like a second mum to me, at least after she got over her initial hunch that I was big trouble and shouldn't be anywhere near her boy. She wasn't entirely wrong, but she saw how me and George were together, and she saw the other side to me too, and so we were all grand and good to go.

I was a bit more streetwise than George; he had the calm and restful home life. We covered for each other, we kept each other safe. I came up with the japes, he had the athleticism to pull them off.

When we were twelve years old, word got round that one of the older kids at our school wanted to beat me up. Rumour was I'd stitched up his little brother, which I hadn't, or at least couldn't remember doing. All day long this chat was going round.

'He's gonna batter you after school, mate. He's outside the gates. You shitting yourself, are ya?'

I was, a bit. I took George aside.

'He's out there, George, he's waiting for me . . .'

'Don't you worry about that, Ronnie, I got a plan.'

'Yeah?'

'Yeah. I'm going out there, and I'm gonna call him a wanker.'

'You what?'

'Yeah. He'll come after me, and then you leg it. Right?'

Now George Palacaros was the best runner in the district. He could run the 100 metres in about twelve seconds. He out-ran the West Ham first team when he was fourteen – him in the junior team, them all training, George streaking away like a bullet.

No one could ever keep up with him. So he shot out of the school gate, gave it the wanker chat, hand gestures, all sorts, and sure enough, the big kid started chasing him and that was it. I got home and George was already there, barely out of breath. Nice one, cheers mate.

I'd always keep an eye out for him after that. If ever he had any trouble, I'd always have his back. We're still mates today; he lives round the corner, he's one of the few people I text back as soon as they text me. But when school finished for us at sixteen, he went off to the US for five years. He was a good footballer, and he went a fair way there. So when Dad went away, and I started coming off the rails more and more, there was no George looking out for me, and there was no hiding away at Lula's.

There was no hiding away at Mum's, after 1995. She had taken over the running of Dad's sex shops with him inside, and the business side of it had never been her thing. She didn't know what she was doing. So they did her on the VAT, and tax evasion, and suddenly I went from having one parent in prison to two of them.

Now that's quite the scenario to find yourself in, when you're nineteen years old and already with the wobbles, and your little sister is twelve, and you don't know how to cook but you've got to look after her too, in this big old house that just feels empty now.

I didn't do a great job. Who would? Making fish fingers and oven chips for Danielle's tea every night, inviting loads of people over each weekend to make the house feel full again, to shove the loneliness away for a few hours.

I was smoking too much weed, I was bulk-buying too much Smirnoff. I'd always been capable of putting away a fair amount of food, as George's mum Lula had found, but now I found new gears. Calling up minicabs and getting them to deliver enough McDonald's to feed most of 'D' wing at the Scrubs, going down the list on the menu for the local Chinese and ordering so much you would struggle to actually take it away.

Sixteen stone, when my natural weight as a late teenager should have been eleven, twelve max. A right old gut on me, my snooker waistcoats straining at the seams, being let out at the back and then abandoned altogether for a larger man's cut. Puffing like a maniac in the evening, lining up the food beforehand, waking up with the munchies and smashing a load more down.

I couldn't cope with my sister. I didn't know how. After six months of me failing and her struggling she went to live with the family of my mum's best mate, and things were straight away much better. She got the nurturing there she needed. She got the looking after I couldn't do.

I needed a family around me too. And I found one, in an unconventional way, when my dad introduced me to a mate of his on the outside called Willy. I met him at King's Cross one morning, and he took me up to Liverpool on the train. You're staying with us, Ronnie. We'll keep an eye on you.

I stayed there for about two years. Me, Willy, his family, all in this little terraced house on an estate in Anfield.

I loved it. I felt safe, within a couple of days. I loved the community, I loved the way people didn't care who you were. Everyone bowling about the streets, in and out of each other's front doors. 'Alright, lad?'

I was still in a bad place, I wasn't able to take care of myself. But I felt looked after and cared for. I wasn't on my own. Some of them would go out to work, I'd go to the local snooker hall and practise. I'd get back to Willy's and he'd order a massive Chinese. All these grand houses in parts of north-east London, and the people inside them shut off from everyone else, not a clue who their neighbours were. Here in Anfield. you knew everyone and everyone knew you. Always someone with a story to tell, always someone looking to have a laugh, never a moan.

I wasn't a talker, back then. You grow up with a dad so loud and charismatic and there's not the space for you to be the same. I used to sit there saying nothing, watching it all unfolding, trying to figure out the angles and links and how to fit in.

I always wanted other people to be happy, even if I wasn't. Maybe because I wasn't. I'd almost shape-shift a little in certain situations, become the person they wanted me to be. When

Dad went away, I became very protective of my mum. If I felt on my own, I reasoned, it must be worse for her. I sensed she needed someone to carry the weight for her, to fill a little of the noise and space left by Dad. She is naturally a thoughtful person, a hospitable person. I absorbed that and tried to reflect it back at her, right up to the point Mum got sent down and I picked up the party baton and went with it.

When she came out of prison, after seven months, she had changed. She had toughened up. A stronger person, with stricter boundaries around herself, with firmer boundaries for me.

I couldn't get away with what I had started doing, not around her. I'd developed relationships with people she didn't like and didn't want in her house. You want to hang around with them lot, Ronnie? You can pack your bags then.

She kicked me out, more than once. I ended up in a random hotel in the Docklands and got into a fight in the boozer over the road. People swinging cues at each other like Stone Age men with clubs. Not really disproving the point Mum was trying to make.

It did make us closer. Both of us with the sense that we needed each other's support. That we had to stick together. If she wasn't doing too well, I would tell her not to worry about it. I've got you covered, Mum. When I was falling, she would try to be there to catch me too. We will get through this. They're not breaking us.

But I did find it hard. The sense of abandonment, the feeling that everything had to be harder for me than everyone else. Going to tournaments as the outsider who everyone stared at. My game getting worse, because how can you be calm and focused when everything around you is relentless drama? My self-esteem collapsing, because I knew my snooker was getting worse, and the snooker was supposed to be keeping Dad happy, and what was the point of any of it if I couldn't do the one thing everyone liked me for doing?

I never felt good about myself. Winning was hollow when I knew I should be playing so much better. Defeat was a disaster, for defeat was not supposed to be an option. I was being forced to grow up faster than I should have done. When you're a kid it's good to be allowed to stay in kid mode for as long as you can. I didn't have that option. I was pushed into a role I felt shouldn't really be my role, and I just had to do it.

You could see it in the way you were treated by your rivals at the big events, hear it in the questions the journalists would ask you afterwards. I felt it from the people running the sport. Right at the start, when Dad had just gone away, the referee Len Ganley came up to me backstage. Everyone loved Len, at least those who hadn't met him. He was the referee you always saw on the telly, the big man with the white gloves and the nice smile.

Well, he wasn't like that behind the scenes. He wasn't liked that way. Me at sixteen years old, him more than thirty years older. Strolling over, giving me a nudge.

'What's your dad's favourite meal, then – a carvery?'

Nice thing to say to a kid whose father is in prison for stabbing a man to death. I shrugged it off, then, because I still felt strong in my game and my head. Had he said the same thing when I was twenty, I probably would have headbutted him, like I headbutted his son Mike at the Worlds in 1996 when he tried throwing me and my mate out of the players' lounge. I'm not proud of it; it's the only headbutt I've ever done in my life, and the only time I've grabbed someone by the balls and called them a grass. Like I say, I'd lost my way. I'd become someone I didn't want to be.

Those were the situations I would find myself in, from 1994 to 2000. From eighteen to twenty-four years old, lost in the woods, raging against the sky. Sometimes I'd have Dad bawling down the phone at me, his voice echoing down the corridors. He's one of those people who can make you believe you can do anything, who can convince you when you think you're already convinced the other way. He can also unload on you if he thinks you're messing up, and at times I needed that tough love. I was naughty. I was a little fucker, too often.

I had to change. I had to get away from the new me, because I hated him, and he had destroyed the old Ronnie.

I had to find myself, too, beyond the shadow of my dad. No one else could be like him. He's like Del Boy from *Only Fools and Horses*, or Joe Pasquale. He's not normal. He's everything dialled up to 200 per cent. And if he's Del Boy, I'm probably Rodney. One the centre of it all, the other watching. One leading the way, the other looking for space to be himself. The optimist and the pessimist, the dreamer and the realist.

He instilled a belief in me that wasn't always there. He had that way about him. He certainly believed in me more often than I believed in myself. It was good for me, but I had to free myself from it too. It's easy to tell someone to go out and perform, a different matter doing it yourself. The trepidation, the fear I experience before every game of snooker? That's all me. No one else who hasn't played at this level understands what that's like.

Am I going to be able to perform today?

That's a line only I get haunted by.

So I don't allow him in now. He stays in the corridors, on the streets outside. Pacing, and scrolling, and shouting.

But I still think about making him feel good. I still think

about him in that jail cell, on his own, watching me on his little portable TV.

Me, the light in the tunnel. Me, his great escape.

Sheffield, 7 May 2001.
World Championship final v John Higgins

A good seventeen days. A solid seventeen days, when you've grown accustomed to wild Ronnie. When you're used to fireworks for a round or two and then capitulation.

10-2 in the first round, 13-6 in the second. Past Peter Ebdon 13-6 in the quarters, past Joe Swail 17-11 in the semi-finals.

Now it's John Higgins in the final. Seven months older than me, world champion three years ago.

Ahead of me on the curve, but not today. I'm a changed man this year, a different man in a different place. I've been to the Priory, I've done my Narcotics Anonymous meetings. I've not touched a spliff since Christmas.

The first year I've come to World Championships and thought, we might as well stay here as long as we can, 'cos I ain't getting smashed after it.

Short hair, side parting, little bit of wax. A sober look.

Monday night at the Crucible, and I'm one frame away. 17-14 up. I should be there already. Frame just gone I was in total control. 63 points ahead, 67 left in on the table, a piss-easy straight red to the middle.

Pot it and Higgins needs two snookers. Pot it and I'm king of the world.

Except I don't, do I? I start making my victory speech in my head. What I'm going to say when the trophy is under my arm and Dougie Donnelly's got his microphone under my nose. Who I'm going to thank, who I'm going to praise.

I start thinking about my dad, in Wormwood Scrubs. Watching on his telly.

I can't believe I actually missed that red. I played it the wrong way as well. Should have just stunned it in, rolled it in. What a twat.

Higgins cleared up, like he always clears up. 17-14, and I could lose this now. Once Higgins gets confident, he can keep you off the table.

And he fancies it alright. Spring in his step, rubbing his hands together. That's the problem – you let them off the hook, and they get confidence from nowhere. Someone like him, you don't want to give him any hope.

I go for a safety off a red. Butcher it.

You're under it now, mate, bang under pressure. I wouldn't be if I was playing someone else; only him and Hendry. Any other player, I could just steady the ship. I'd get a chance. Higgins and Hendry? You might not get another chance.

Sitting back in me chair. Fuck me, Ronnie, this could be career-ending shit.

How am I going to get over this? How am I going to explain to people that it wasn't pressure why I missed the red? Are they going believe I was thinking about the speech? They're going to think I'm making excuses again . . . Sitting here, chewing the inside of my mouth. Lean forward, so he doesn't think I'm thinking I'm out of this.

Higgins with the pots. Smooth. Hungry. Easy up to 38 points, 45 with a black that wobbles in the left corner but drops. If he goes 17-15 here, I am bang under the truck. I could lose.

Straight red to the same pocket . . . He should never have missed that. Not with his cue action.

Right. On your feet, Ronnie.

I've got to clear up otherwise I am fucked. If I don't clear up here, he's going to ruin me.

You've learned now, yeah? One ball at a time, just pot, pot, keep focused, pot.

Stop thinking about speeches. Don't even make a speech, just win. Just stay in the present.

Red, black. Red, black.

Bit of a bail-out shot on that red to the left middle, bit of a bottle shot. Get the rest out for the yellow, take the red to the left baulk corner and back for the blue.

45 plays 25.

Keep it steady. Sacrifice speed for being clinical.

Blue goes, white on to cannon off the two reds near the pink spot.

I don't feel hurried now. My bridge hand feels good.

On the rest, taking on the red to right corner and staying nice for the pink.

Higgins knows now. He's pulling at his bottom lip.

My lines are good, my cue ball control is good. I'm keeping it tight, stroking the ball nice.

Red tucked behind the black, need the white to keep going here, get me the angle.

Yep. Ahead in the frame. Black goes, further ahead.

I ain't missing really. Don't think so. Last red in centre right, nice angle on the blue for the yellow.

60 points plays 45. A glance at the scoreboard.

I need yellow, green and brown.

Murmurs in the crowd as the yellow goes. Easy on the green. Deep breaths all around.

Bang straight on the brown.

Sink it.

Massive roar from the crowd. Bite me lip. Round for the blue, crowd still cheering and whistling.

Stay in the moment here, Ronnie. You've done this loads of times.

Just stay in the moment, just stay in the moment.

Drop my cue on the table. Hands on my head. Shake Higgins's hand.

God, it's pure relief. Pure relief.

I thought I might never win this tournament. I could go my whole career without winning it.

Now it's done. The pressure, it's done.

It's over.

I celebrated that night like I'd never celebrated before: by sitting there drinking Perrier water while Jimmy White and Ronnie Wood were having fun in the room upstairs.

I'll be honest: if my mum hadn't been with me, I would have been up there with them like a shot. Out of the Priory and into the fire. It's hard not to go back to the old ways when you've just won your first world title. You only win your first one once, why not go for it?

Instead, I went to bed about half one, two. And I slept well, because it wasn't excitement I was feeling. It was still that relief. Thank God I've got it out of the way.

I had lost so many semi-finals, blown so many chances. I thought maybe my chance had gone. Those seven years where I smashed myself to pieces were not coming back. It's better, with something epic like the Worlds, to get it out of the way as early as you can and then crack on. I'd left it late. I was twenty-five years old and I should have been twenty-one.

Twenty-five doesn't seem quite as old now I'm forty-seven. But when you're twenty-five, you're thinking that Hendry stopped winning tournaments at thirty-two, that Davis stopped winning tournaments at thirty-two. You think, I've only got a seven-year window here to get anything else done.

At twenty-five I was still doing it for my dad. For him inside, for Mum backstage in Sheffield. Keeping an eye on me after. At forty-seven I'm a parent myself, and it changes how I look at the way they were with me, at how they are today.

I see my dad quite a bit these days. We talk, we chat on the phone. I enjoy checking in with him. He's become much better at realising when to back off from me. He knows what I'm like, he's good at judging my mood. And I am a lot better at understanding that as parents we just do our best.

My relationship with my kids is different to how it was for me and Mum and Dad. I haven't been the best parent in the world, not all from my own failings, but I have missed out. I don't see Taylor-Ann; I was never part of her life, and I've had to accept that. With Lily and Ronnie junior, I haven't been able to be a hands-on dad, and that has been more difficult to cope with.

I got caught between two immovable demands, in their early days. The relationship with their mother Jo broke down. I was the breadwinner, so I had to earn the money, but my job can never be a nine to five. You have to travel to play; tournaments finish at weekends, to maximise TV audiences. Often I had to choose between playing snooker and seeing my kids, and I had to play to pay for their house, and maintenance, and education.

For two years I put the playing second. I missed a lot of competitions, but I wanted to create a bond with them, so I don't regret doing it. The problems came when their mother and I couldn't agree on the dates when each of us were in charge. The year I was supposed to choose, according to our settlement, it didn't happen, and we ended up in court, and I lost.

That was it. I walked out of that court with no path open to me but getting on with life on my own. I thought, I'll get my head down and do what I've got to do. I'll earn the money to pay their bills, pay their school fees, look after them financially for the first eighteen years. If I get to see them, it'll be great. If I don't, I've still got to get on with it.

It was hard. I had to grow a thicker skin again. I thought: Ronnie, what sort of parent are you going to be if you're fragile and unable to cope? You're better off being strong, seeing them less but still remaining in some sort of relationship with them, so when they do come to you, you've got something about you, you're not a broken man anymore.

I'd rather die than be on my knees living. That's how I felt.

I struggled with it for a long time. I wanted to see Lily and Ronnie but there was no flexibility to allow me to do so and also stay within snooker's random demands. Financially it was a stress. I couldn't afford to put all my eggs in one basket and rely upon prize money. Snooker's too hard, too competitive. I had to take on additional jobs, more secure sources of income – my punditry with Eurosport, ambassador deals, exhibition matches. They helped with the income, and they helped with my sanity. I couldn't play snooker thinking of the money. I was never a money player. I was always a competition player.

So this is where we are, today. I missed out on the front end of their parenting, and I've tried to cope with it by hoping I might get the back end, as they get old enough to make their own minds up. Maybe they thought I was a jerk, maybe they think I am a jerk. But they're still young, and they have so much time ahead. We have a long time to be together. I can be a friend to them, rather than an authority figure. I hope they will come to me for advice, and support.

I see a lot of myself in Lily. She's hard on herself, always striving for excellence. She gets stressed out by her school, her exams, her running. She puts her heart and soul into everything, yet she'll often think she's not good enough, when she clearly is.

I worry for her. I don't want her to end up like me. It took me long enough to work it out for myself, but all the success in the world is not worth it if you're not able to enjoy it. O'Sullivan lesson number one.

Ronnie junior's more laid back. He's like a little surfer, an Aussie boy. He's happy, he's good-looking. Nothing appears to faze him. He takes it all in his stride, and that's lovely to me. I wish I could be more like him.

Lily has the fighting spirit, the sense of competition that I do. Ronnie doesn't need the fighting spirit. He doesn't get obsessed, like us. He just lets everything wash over him, which is the best way to be.

They can share in what I do, now. The pleasure of a father showing his kids the world he moves through, the obsessions and dreams that have worked for him.

I shared it with them when I won the world title in 2012. The two of them with me by the table in the aftermath, confetti in their hair, trophy in their hands. Ronnie in my arms with his smart red trousers and grey T-shirt and floppy fringe. A year before, thinking I was finished, working out the retirement speech. Then meeting Steve Peters, beginning to play the best snooker I've ever played. A moment I never thought would happen, a moment I could share with them. The snooker gods looking at us all and saying – yes mate, you can have this one, you've earned it.

Ten years on, and they came up again for the final day of the 2022 championships. I struggled in the afternoon session, and I felt terrible about it. I felt embarrassed my kids had seen me fall apart. I took my daughter aside before the evening session.

'Lily, I'm so sorry.'

'Dad, what you on about? I don't care. Just do your best, I don't care if you win or lose.'

'Really?'

'Yeah! We'd love you to win, but as long as you enjoy it, that's all good.'

'Really? We can have a good night together whether I win or lose, but . . .'

'Dad, enjoy it. You can do this.'

Imagine hearing that. I went out into that final session, and the magic came back and I won, and all I was thinking was: they're happy I made the final, they're happy if I'm happy, and we're all here, doing it together.

They saw their dad out there grafting and they saw me playing as well as I could. They saw me delivering under the most extreme pressure I ever experienced. And while it was wonderful a decade before, it was even more special to have them there as teenagers. Understanding the game, feeling the magnitude of it all. Them watching their dad and feeling proud.

When I did see them when they were smaller, I loved doing sporty things with them. Passing on that lovely habit. We'd get the bikes out, fill the rucksack up with sandwiches, pile over to the forest, get them muddy, get them dirty . . . all of it an adventure. At first, they'd be all complaints – don't want to do this, can't we watch telly? Twenty minutes later, mud all over their faces, they'd be telling me how much they loved it. I wanted the time they spent with me to be in the fresh air, away from technology, no need for mobiles and tablets and that sort of nonsense. I'd take Lily running in the forest. She was good, proper good. Speed and endurance and absolutely the guts for it all.

Now they're older and they come over to the house, it can

be harder – not because their personalities have changed, and I don't want to do the same things, but because they begin to look at the world in a different way. I'm not a day-to-day parent; it's weekends, and little bursts in the holidays. Sometimes I don't know what they'd like to do. Sometimes I'd say things to them and I wouldn't find out until a week later that I'd said the wrong thing. I wouldn't know what my son liked to eat. I didn't know them well enough.

And that hurts, of course it does. All of us. Now I try to ask more questions. I give them more freedom. What do you fancy tonight? Why don't you order the pizzas? I'll give you the money, you be in charge.

The two of them have their own lives. I can't be the pushy parent, not least because I'm not there enough to pick them up when they fall down. I have to support, I have to be there for them. Not turn them into me.

And that's the big thing, if you want to take something from all of this for yourself. You aren't your parents, and your kids aren't you. Take them as they are. Give them the room to become themselves. And give them the time so you can get to know the real them too.

The best thing you can ever do for your kids is to help them identify their passion and then follow it into adult life. It's hard to work out what you want to do when you're sixteen, when you're thinking of leaving school and going out into the world, and so the temptation for parents can be to map your kids' lives out for them. Part of me wants to do that for mine. It's a way of protecting them, of trying to future-proof an uncertain time.

But when I listen to successful people – not successful in the way you might think, with big houses and flash cars and all that, but people who are happy for long periods of time – it often comes back to finding what you love. I've listened to

Stephen Fry talking about how he hated chasing a rugby ball around the school playing fields, how he would hide away in a corner of the library reading books instead. He said that words brought him alive, and I love that, because that's what snooker did for me, when I was the same age.

Tune in to the things that spark your children. Maybe it's the same thing as you, but it's often not. And when you see them come alive – when you see that look in their eyes, or hear them talking to their friends about it, and they want to share it with you too – that's when you encourage them to do more of it. You might not know it yourself when you're younger, but you have freedom at that age. If you get to your mid-twenties and the passion play isn't working out, you can change tack then, choose a job that keeps you secure and still leaves time for the lifestyle you want to live. Until then? That's the time to take risks. That's the time to be mindful of their talents. To feed the spark.

I love it when I see my kids with their nan and their grandad now, getting to know my side of their family. They think my dad is mad, funny, all laughs. My mum just dotes on them. They love going round to hers because they get well fed and they can put their feet up without getting their heads pecked. They are well loved by their grandparents, and they love their grandparents as well.

Life isn't easy as a parent. That's what you realise, when you do it yourself. You're not perfect. You have tired days and grumpy days and plenty of days when you just get it wrong. My parents are as much of an accidental product of the way they were raised as I am. My dad is still the kid that grew up in Hackney when you didn't want to grow up in Hackney, the kid who used to wear his sister's old clothes because his mum couldn't afford to buy him his own. He still can't stand it if I throw something away. He thinks it's frivolous.

Mum is exactly the same. Her parents were immigrants from Sicily. They had nothing. She had to cook for all her brothers. She's paid off her mortgage and she's got a property portfolio bigger than mine, and she will still keep the same car for twenty years. She'll still make soup out of the leftovers and pop to Oxfam when she needs clothes.

Understanding them has helped me understand me. I can't spend £100 on sunglasses, I can't work out how someone spends £500 on a pair of shoes. When my clothes are falling apart, I just go to Marks and buy five pairs of shorts and five T-shirts and I'm happy. I spent a whole year living on a barge, back in 2009. I enjoyed it.

And we got through it, in the end. Mum and Dad got divorced when he came out of prison, but that was for the best. They are both financially okay. He paved the way for us to have a nice life with all he earned before he went away; me and Mum worked hard to keep it good for him when he came back. Mum's got her house, and she's happy. Dad bowls about in his campervan, and he loves the freedom of being able to go wherever he wants to go, whenever he likes. And that makes sense too.

I don't see my sister a great deal anymore. I feel for her. I think she's had a tough life. I feel for her more than anybody in my family, because she was even younger than I was when our dad and my mum went away. I don't think she got the guidance that she needed, but she is a survivor. She is strong. She knows if ever she needs me, I am there. She knows she's got my mum, she's got Dad. She just does her own thing.

Dad? He's fundamentally the same person he always was. He hasn't lost his spirit or his sense of humour. He has just become more accepting of things. When he first came out, I think he had ambitions of getting back to where he had been in business, but the world had changed a lot. I would have hated it if after twenty years inside he had nothing, that he was sleeping on sofas. But he's okay. He's still . . . him.

He said something to me the other day, too. Something I'm not going to forget.

'Ronnie, I've realised how good you was.'

'What do you mean?'

'I used to be . . . when you won a match, I was like, That's it, let's get on to the next one.'

'I know.'

'Now YouTube's come along, I've started watching a lot of your old matches. And I've watched all of your matches, instead of just seeing you get over the line.'

'Really?'

'Yeah. And fuck me, you was good. You are good . . .'

9

RUNNING
ALWAYS IN MY MIND

Here's me, first thing on a dark November morning.

Alarm going off at 6.15 a.m. Opening my eyes to one thought. *What the hell am I doing getting out of bed at this time?*

Takes me a second or two to remember I've got the best reason in the world. I'm going running with my mates Greg and Sonny. Out in nature with two lovely people who give you the best sort of energy. And I'll say to them when I meet them, round the back of the shops, in the unpretentious little Ilford Athletic Club Portakabins: no matter what else happens in the next fifteen hours, coming here and meeting you and having a run has made it a great day.

Now it's never easy getting up at that time. The first part is always the hardest. It's dark in the house. Laila is asleep. Osho is asleep in his basket. You might hear a podcast coming out of a speaker somewhere, and it may freak you out, thinking someone else is awake at this time, but it's just playing on from when I stuck it on in the middle of the night to get me through my insomnia.

It's easy to make excuses with the insomnia. Well, I haven't slept great, so really I should lie in for another couple of hours, and even if I am just resting, it's better than getting out of bed and taking the day on before I'm ready. But I'll never make it that way. Steve Peters always says to me: when you get out of bed, it's the overthinking that does it. Just count your first ten steps instead.

One. First step out of bed. Two, three, four to the bathroom. Five, six, seven to the sink. Eight, nine, bedroom door. Ten, top of the stairs.

Once I'm brushing my teeth I'm usually up and away. There's no turning back then. If I can't make that first step, I think about getting to the kettle and making a cup of tea.

Ronnie, just turn that kettle on, get the milk out the fridge, and you'll be out the front door five minutes later.

If I lie in bed thinking about getting to the car and going for a run, I could be two hours. I can sit there and talk myself out of it. You've got to trick yourself sometimes. Get the cuppa down me, then I'm in a better position to make a sensible decision. Let's get our kitbag ready and we're out the door.

Ten minutes across the empty streets in north-east London in the car. Towel and spare clothes in my bag. Park up at the gates, see the boys, pull my trainers on.

A couple of minutes into the run, my legs are moving and the blood's pumping. The whole of Hainault Forest to ourselves, or that's what it feels like. Soft light and dew in summer, frozen ground and crunchy grass in winter. I breathe deep and think, Yeah, this is great. This is the best thing for me.

I hated running at school. When it was cross-country day in PE I'd call a taxi from the payphone and get it to come and collect me so I could swerve the exercise.

'Mate, ask the driver to go right through the school gates please, right up to the front door.'

I'd dive in the passenger door, get my head down and tell

them to get the hell out of Dodge, because there would be two teachers on guard duty by the gates, and if they saw O'Sullivan's chubby face sticking out of a minicab I'd be in a right load of trouble.

That was me. I was the fat kid that didn't want to run for the ball even when we played football. And this is me thirty years later: a running bore who's got loads of friends on Strava and likes chatting the nuances of a good off-road 10k and bigging up a stranger for their new Parkrun PB.

It keeps me accountable, these early starts to meet Greg and Sonny. If I wasn't looking forward so much to their company, I might not get to the kettle and the cuppa. Once I'm in the rhythm of things and I'm fit and running seven and eight miles without a sweat I can make myself do it. But the tough sessions need other strong people around you.

It's the same as playing against Mark Williams and John Higgins. As being beaten by Stephen Hendry. They've made me want to be better. It's a good thing for all of us to be around people who do this to us.

I've used people in a healthy way to push myself on. I'm not driven by the trophies, or the cash. I honestly don't care about being well known or rated by others. But I love that form of healthy competition. Looking those players in the eye, shaking their hands all serious, and smiling inside. It's a privilege for you and me to be here today playing against each other. When we were kids we would both have been dreaming about matches and days like these.

You can lose sight of your roots when you're lost in the minutiae of a season. When I was ten years old even the thought of playing at the Crucible was incredible to me. Now I've won the world title there seven times the simplest way I can appreciate it is to go back to that kid commentating to himself as he played shots because he never imagined he was ever going to be play-ing on TV. To be out there competing with these top players for so long is a reason to be happy and content. Who gives a monkey's about the result when you're doing what you always dreamed of doing?

A lot of me getting out of bed so early, starting my day out in the woods and under the leaves, is based around that same sense of healthy competition. Take that away from me and I pretty quickly become a lazy bastard. When I gave up snooker for a year in 2013, I thought I would be able to do two sessions of exercise a day – a run after breakfast, some strength work in the gym in the afternoon. I was deluded. Within a couple of weeks, I was staying in bed until eleven in the morning. Some-times midday. I wasn't managing even one session of training.

I had no structure to my life. Steve Peters spotted it. Ronnie, we all need a sense of purpose. I thought, you're right. I am one of them. I need a mission and then I am up for the mission. It's why I ended up taking a job volunteering at the farm in Hainault Forest. It made me accountable. Okay, work starts at 9 a.m., so I'll have to be in the forest for 8 a.m. so I can get my morning run in.

You run and you compete. I love the social and the spiritual side and I love the thrill of racing too. Pinning a number to your vest, pushing yourself harder than you ever thought pos-sible. Finishing wherever you finish, shaking hands with the geezer who's finished just in front of you and the one who's finished just behind.

I was lucky I found it in the first place. I was coming off one of my benders, sometime in the summer of 2004, still bloated from the late-night spliffs and the later-night munchies. Down the gym trying to work it all out of my system. Motivated by guilt and shame and embarrassment. Trudging along on the treadmill, barely moving it. Starting a conversation with a mate of mine, Alan, who was training alongside me. Twenty-odd years older than me, but a proper runner, as it turns out.

He invited me for a run in the forest. Yeah, why not, Alan? I've got nothing else to do but dig out the Rizlas and mong about on the sofa watching Sky Sports News. We did five miles around Hainault that day, and I was knackered, but he was fresh as a daisy. I couldn't work out how he'd done it. Five miles was so far. Hainault Forest is not a flat place.

He told me about the running club. Woodford Green at that point, all history and class. I went down to the track for the Tuesday night training session and from that moment on, that was it.

Everything was done on the whistle. A big old group of mixed abilities, so no set distance reps, all based on time. A whistle to go, a whistle to stop. A lot of quality runners from back in the day – forty- and fifty-year-olds who had run sub thirty minutes for 10k in their pomp and were still banging out thirty-five minutes now. An experienced group dragging me along, offering help and encouragement on every rep and on each additional week I turned up.

We'd meet at 6.30 p.m. at the track in Ashton Park, right next to the M11. You could see it as you came south on the motorway. The brightness of the floodlights, the reddish brown of the track. The white paint of the lanes and the dark green infield.

No one ever spoke about anyone's job. No one badgered me about my snooker or came up with a critique of the way I'd played a safety at the English Open. It was purely about running: the session we were going to do, the races coming up, what was on at the weekend.

It was a whole new world to me, and it was brilliant. We'd

warm up, do our running drills. Then we'd begin the session. I started at the back, but as each week went by I would make small incremental improvements and get slightly closer to the person in front. Miraculously, you'd then overtake a few. You would work your way through the pack. Start further towards the front, picking better runners off each week.

You learned to judge yourself by the quality of the runner you could stay close to. Someone like Johnny Wallis, a fantastic runner and good lad. Another guy called Billy Wootton, a proper good footballer as a kid and now, in his fifties, banging out ten-milers in forty-nine minutes. On good nights I could get up to him and on great nights I'd suddenly be running alongside him, and it all felt magical and impossible and as intoxicating as any drug I'd ever lobbed down my neck. Then we'd finish the session, do our warm-down, have a shower and pile into the bar area, where everyone was on the orange squash. We'd talk races, we'd talk times. At 10 p.m. everyone would go home, and I'd get back in my car and think, I feel fantastic, and I've had a bloody good night, and I've only done stuff that's good for me.

That's when it all changed. That's when the penny dropped. I was twenty-nine years old. I had been through rehab for a while at this point. I'd done the Twelve Steps and I thought I'd cracked it, on the basis I could often go three months without a drink or sniff of weed. Occasionally I'd manage six months. But no matter how long, it would always end the same way – a massive night out, all sorts going on, a bigger sense of regret however many days later I came out of it.

Running changed all that. I didn't want to fall off the wagon because I wanted to be up in the morning to do my running. From seeing the sun come up lying on the sofa with pizza crusts on my belly to being out in the forest as dawn kicked in, birds hanging about in the trees, mud and dust under my feet, mates by my side.

I often thought about that night in Holland. The one when I thought I was dying. Paranoid, wasted, lost. I'd be in the woods or burning round the top bend at the track, and I'd think, I've gone from that to this?

The Narcotics Anonymous meetings had been my community. Somewhere to go in the evening when snooker practice was done and I was on my own and the demons started tapping me on the shoulder.

Running became the same thing only better. The club nights were a social thing and a fitness thing and a place I was accepted as exactly who I was. A community that reminded me of those two years in the mid-1990s, living with Willy and his family in Liverpool.

I felt safe, and I hadn't felt safe in a long time. Ever since Liverpool I had appreciated what being embedded in a community can do for you. It's companionship and it's support. It's feeling like you belong.

I still felt lonely at snooker tournaments. I couldn't let my guard down. Everyone looking for flaws and weaknesses. Half of them talking behind my back.

At Woodford Green there was no need to have your guard up. No one went on the piss and no one saw you as a source of free drinks and easy entry into a club. If anyone told you what to do, it was all about making you a better runner.

I had grown up in snooker culture. My heroes were snooker players, my favourite places snooker halls. I fell in love with running in the same way – the distinct smell of an artificial track, the fiddly technical parts like deciding between a 9 mm spike for your race or a 12 mm one. New heroes like Ethiopia's Olympic 10,000-metre champion Kenenisa Bekele and his compatriot Tirunesh Dibaba. I loved that Bekele had won six World Cross-Country titles on the bounce. I was watching in 2008 when his shoe came off mid-race and you thought he was done for. Him stopping all calmly to put it back on, me assuming he was out of the race, because you can't give the best Kenyan athletes thirty seconds and expect to catch them up, and him just working his way back, picking them all off and still winning by a comfortable distance.

This geezer is unbelievable . . .

I felt part of the real British scene. I noticed in one race that a training group in Basildon had taken all six places. It was coached by Eamonn Martin, an elite endurance runner in his day, winner of the London Marathon the first year he ever ran it. So I went and asked if I could join his group.

Running being running, he invited me in. For three months I trained harder than I had ever trained before: hills on a Monday, kilometre reps on the Saturday. It was probably a two-hour round trip in the car, but I loved it, and I was flying. There was no other sport I could think of where you could just turn up and train with the best group around. It was special.

Almost inadvertently it sorted out my weight issues. I'd always been on the chubby side, even before the spliffs, even in what should have been my skinny teenage years. I'd lost weight before as an adult and then always put it back on again, because there was never any consistency in my training. As bingey in that as I was in everything else.

Joining the running club took all the worry out of it. I could carry on eating, which is one of my pleasures in life, and it never went on my belly and arse. I had running friends to meet; I had races to do. It was no longer: Am I going to train, am I not going to train? It was a done deal.

Because of how my brain works, I didn't mess about on the

fringes. I didn't dabble with my new hobby. I threw myself into it proper. I developed such a good network of friends through running and such a clean and easy source of good moods that I didn't want to go away anymore. I began missing tournaments so I could make Tuesday evenings running in the forest.

Very Ronnie. All or nothing. Never bothering with the in-between.

December came round and I was due to play the UK Championship. Not really one you want to miss. So I had a word with one of the lads down the club.

'Mate, I gotta go to Telford. You know anyone up there who would run with me?'

'Let me make some enquiries, Ronnie . . .'

It was the best thing I ever did. He got in contact with the local running club, they hooked me up with a couple of their regulars. And every tournament I went to after that, we'd do the same trick. Email the local running club, put the feelers out.

'I'll be staying in your neck of the woods between these dates. I fancy running between 7.30 a.m. and 8.30 a.m., probably looking at 7 minute 30 seconds per mile pace. If anyone's happy to run that pace with me, I'd love to see them.'

What a win! No matter where I went, I had a portable running community around me. I was staying fit and staying happy. I wasn't worrying so much about the snooker because by the time I got to the table I'd already achieved something cool in the day. And when I got back to north-east London again my fitness was good enough to keep up with the group.

They say most of us can count our true friends on one hand. Through running round the snooker circuit, I must have twenty. Telford means Chris. Llandudno is Martin. Sheffield, Jason; Belfast, Eamon and his crew. John in Newport, brilliant guy; Gary in Milton Keynes, so many good times. In Tring, Phil, Jamie and the two Adams. Friends for life.

Always in my heart, always in my mind. As long as I'm running, and they're running, we seem to connect. It's strange and it's beautiful.

My favourite races were always cross-country. My favourite ever result, based on what I was up against, came in the Metropolitan League up the road at Claybury Park: up against the best cross-country runners north of the Thames, a proper course with mud and hills and the feeling in your guts that a puke was only one more minute of effort away.

The first time I ran in the Met League I finished 200th. Then it was 185th, then 150th.

By the time of this one in the winter of 2007 I'd been running hard for a few years. I was fit – skinnier than I'd ever been, eating heaps and burning off every bowl of porridge and piece of toast I ate. That was the day I finished 53rd.

All the old boys down the club had been telling me that when you run your best races it feels easy. At Claybury I felt like I could keep going forever. Spikes on, the little shorts, the green and white hooped vest of Woodford Green.

A couple of months later I finished 28th at the Essex Cross-Country championships in Basildon. A few weeks after that, I ran the Southerns at Parliament Hill north London, maybe the most famous course on the British scene, and an authentic beast of a race – up, down, up, down, running through streams, quagmires, all sorts. I was 189th there out of about 1,200.

I'd always get nervous, no matter how big the race was. Same as before every snooker match. I didn't mind it. It's natural, when you're putting yourself on the line. Do it often enough and you realise the tension is at its peak just before you begin, and within 200 metres, or three shots, you're away and free.

I began to appreciate the adrenaline they triggered, and I loved the battles within the battles. The top boys were flying machines, capable of banging out twenty-seven minutes for 10k. I never got amongst those, but you would get used to familiar faces at your level.

Ah, he beat me last time, he was just behind, he done me in a sprint for the line.

I used to latch on to certain runners and see how long I could hold on to them for. That was my favoured tactic. Steady on the first lap, push it on the second, dig in on the third. A couple of times I tried to go out hard and then I'd blow up, and when you're dying two miles into a six-mile race it's an awful long slog home from there.

You learn to respect your limits. I learned to push it on the hills, because that was where I could do a bit of damage. All those early-morning runs round the trails of Hainault and Epping served me well. I could get past runners who were better than me on the road or on the track. A bit of Ronnie guts.

We're all hurting here, we're all trying our nuts off. I feel like I'm dying, so you must feel like you're dying too, or else you would have passed me.

All of us out there thanks to the others around us. All pushing each other along, all sweaty hugs at the end. A community of the muddy and exhausted and ecstatic.

I left running alone, after that period, for about ten years. I got injured. Little niggles that became bigger niggles and longer-term problems. Groin, hip, calves. Stress fractures.

Running injured is horrible. You chafe against it and you miss all those endorphins that used to keep you so high. It was only really the Covid pandemic in 2020 and 2021 that got me started again, when our tournaments were being played in

Milton Keynes due to lockdown. I was staying at Champneys in Tring, and I just began plodding round some of the lovely quiet roads and paths round there. It's tough when you're not fit and you're out on your own and you're not moving well. I felt like a hairy slug. I felt embarrassed to run with anyone else; I couldn't go far enough or fast enough to warrant wasting their time.

But it comes back, and it comes back more rapidly if you've been there before. A few months in, out with new running friends, I remembered. I was me again. It felt like it did when I had first taken it up. It set me up for the whole day. I would be careering along the trails thinking, I am so lucky to have running back in my life again.

I ran for a year. I ran for a year and a half. I even entered a Met League race again, over in Welwyn Garden City. Turning up, seeing all these elite athletes warming up, wondering what the hell I was doing amongst them. Pulling my spikes on for the first time in forever, having no idea how far we had to go or what pace I was running. Having to pant to the bloke next to me – we on the last lap, or is there another one to come?

A terrible feeling at the time and a sweet rush afterwards. The pleasure in pinning a number to my vest again, in sorting out the right length spikes. The smell of the mud, the way the course got churned up by each additional race. Watching the youngsters going round, then the women, getting pumped up by seeing them galloping round the course. Barely able to walk properly for the next three days, my calves lacking any condition for wearing spikes. But all the camaraderie and community back again, the same warm sense of belonging. You won't find many arseholes in the running community, that's the thing. It's a great leveller. If you've got an ego and you're a runner, you'll be a lonely person.

In a strange way the peak of my first wave of obsession with running could get in the way of my snooker. I became more interested in getting my run done than going to the practice table. Sometimes I would be too physically tired to play snooker. All those miles in my legs and nothing left for getting in and out of my chair, round the table, up and down into my stance.

But I didn't mind. I gained so much more in health and happiness and inner peace. I wasn't prepared to give all that up to be a better snooker player. Running had saved my life. Whatever I got out of snooker was a bonus.

And really, when I got the balance right, running taught me so much about how to deal with my snooker. It's weird, in some ways, how a sport I took up near my thirtieth birthday has helped me cope with the one I'm meant to be really good at.

You always taper for a race, when you're training properly. You gradually drop off the distance and intensity ahead of your target day to leave yourself fresh for when it really matters. I'd never done that for snooker. No one had. And yet putting my cue down for a week before a big tournament turned out to be beneficial, even if it was counter-intuitive.

Snooker isn't a physical sport in the same way as running. It taxes you mentally instead. The runner's legs are the snooker player's brain. You can put it under stress, but you need to leave time for adaptation to take place as well.

When I come back to snooker after the end-of-season hiatus each year I build up my hours on the practice table, and when I'm up to doing back-to-back six-hour days I take time away to recover. It doesn't mean that I'm getting lazy or not putting the work in. I'm just being smart. Data driven but in a spiritual way. The mind rests and comes back to the game.

Running also allowed me to put snooker on the back-burner sometimes. The relationships it created made me feel good and happy so there was a buffer in place if the snooker went wrong.

Snooker was my job, but the professional world has always left me feeling alienated. If you come to a snooker tournament you won't see me at the venue outside my matches. You don't see me hanging around with other players. Not because I don't like them, but because I have nothing in common with them.

In Sheffield I'm up at seven in the morning going running through the valleys and the mountains. They're sitting there drinking, playing cards and talking about snooker until midnight or one in the morning, and then they're at the venue talking about rankings and tournaments and politics in snooker. I just don't want to be around that. I find it boring in comparison to the empty trails and early-morning skies.

Running allowed me to switch off and not even think about snooker. I am fine with having a match ahead of me to play at seven in the evening. I know that when I put my suit on, something inside me will say, right, we're going to work. I will switch on. Now it's time to play.

All the hours until then are mine. Running, having breakfast with my running mates, in a coffee bar, eating good food. Before I found running I'd be down at the venue, practising, hanging around the hotel, eating too much, hanging out with the other players. That all disappeared the day I bought my first pair of running shoes.

For the last twenty years I've probably been the most antisocial snooker player on the circuit. One of the players said to me recently: we call you the Ghost. We never see you, but we always know about ten minutes before your game you'll slip in and then as soon as you're done, you're gone, you're out. You're not the Rocket. You're the Ghost.

I've got zero interest in being around snooker people. It's a shame, in some regards, but I suppose that's what happens when you find a love for something else. It's a little like John

McEnroe. He strikes me as someone who would rather have been an artist or guitarist than a tennis player. It's just his talent was on a court.

So it's an easy lesson from me, this one. Run. Walk if you can't. Keep going.

You don't have to think of yourself as a runner. I never was. Just begin. Leave the front door and see where it takes you. It could be somewhere pretty special.

Try your local parkrun. They're amazing things – 9 o'clock on a Saturday morning, in so many places around the country, a free 5k you can race, jog or walk. A lovely community of supportive people, the best way to start your weekend.

And if you can't run, and don't want to walk, find the place that does for you what Hainault Forest and Epping Forest and various hidden trails and hills round the country do for me. You can't always work things out in your own head. That's what snooker and everything around it has taught me. So go to the place where you can switch off, where you won't be hassled and you don't feel stressed.

Maybe it's the cinema. It might be a quiet place where you can read a good book in peace. Maybe it's a little trip to Waitrose to get yourself a few goodies for later.

Sometimes, if you're really busy, it can just be putting things in your diary to look forward to. That always makes me feel happier. A trip away in a month's time, a meal you're going to cook. The thought of lunch with an old friend might be enough to get you through a bad day.

If you fancy something else? Life is as much about recovery as hard effort. When you're under stress, the body and mind won't allow adaptations to take place. Stay calm and relaxed, let yourself rest. I had a week off before the World Championship in 2012, and look what happened there.

I would love to run the London Marathon one day. I'm not going to be doing what Eamonn Martin did but I'd love to have a go at it and experience all the things I've been told about.

For now, I need to keep the injuries at bay. That's where I am with my running today, as the alarm goes off and I climb out of bed and begin counting those first ten steps. I love running with a torch in my hand, starting in the dark, running towards the light. An easy metaphor for all of us to get our heads around.

I try to keep my heart-rate low when I'm out with Greg and Sonny. Get the miles in, build up the weeks of training. As long as I'm not trying to break records all over the gaff, I've got a shot.

I'd love to race again. Pull on a vest, pin on a number. Get out there in the mud and the hills and the sharp elbows and smell of it all.

Even if I can't train hard, I'll still be up early, and I'll still be out in the forest. Striding out, sucking in the fresh air. Getting a sweat on and accepting the pace I'm running that day. Not needing to consciously figure things out, just waiting for the answers to come to me. Having a stretch, having a shower. Feeling better than I did before.

Everything sorted out, naturally.

10

CONNECTING
THE BUDDHIST MONK
OF SNOOKER

This is me, Tuesday morning, just before Christmas, at home.

I've been for my run. Groin was a bit sore, and it was dark and cold when I met Greg and Sonny, but I warmed up after the first twenty minutes. Forty minutes in I was cruising. And by the time we'd done our eight miles and had the hot showers and got ourselves into the café for a nice bowl of porridge, all was ticking along and you could forget the rain outside and feel good about all that had come before and all that might come later.

It's being part of something that is bigger than me, the morning run. It's connecting to other people. Sometimes you talk about big stuff, and it's easy because you're running together, and feeling the same way, and in step emotionally as well as physically. Other times you feel better from just talking about other things. Sharing and listening.

That's how it is with Greg, a man with an amazing heart. I love his story, I love where he's come from, I love what he is doing. I love the resilience he is living by. Sometimes when I'm talking to him it feels like I've got David Seaman on my side. A safe pair of hands whatever gets thrown at us.

Now I'm back home. Warm coat on, old trainers, Osho ready for his walk in the park across the road. Belt round my waist with poo bags and a little sack of dog treats for when Osho brings the ball back from wherever I've lobbed it.

No one bothers us when we're over there. I'm just a man with a dog, to the other men and women with dogs we might bump into. That's what we'll talk about, if we stop at all. How old is yours? Isn't she lovely? Here, is yours allowed one of these? Another connection with someone who might otherwise be a stranger.

Something happened to me on the way back from my run. Something that happens a fair amount. I was in my Smart car – tiny little thing, two seats only, ideal for the busy streets and heavy traffic and no parking spaces round here. I was waiting at a red light. Two lanes of traffic, and the bloke in the car alongside me glances over, and then looks back and stares – at my face, at the car, at my face again. And his expression was a familiar one: What are you, *you*, doing in that thing?

Because the world is a weird place, sometimes, when the world thinks it recognises you. When it thinks it knows everything about you.

If I could be the best snooker player ever and no one else knew anything about it or anything about me, I would be perfectly happy.

That would be pure snooker, in my head. Pure snooker was me as a kid, as an amateur, when the insiders at the clubs knew me but no one else had a clue. No politics, no nonsense, no being told you're bringing the game into disrepute. Okay, I got banned from a Pontins holiday camp when I was ten years old, but that was because I was being chased by a big kid called Fast Eddie, and I threw a glass on the floor to put him off, and an old dear thought I'd thrown it at her, which I definitely didn't, and stuff happened as a result. But anyway.

I have absolutely no interest in being famous. I have no interest in being a celebrity or in people who are celebrities. There was a part of me that, after my seventh world title in 2022, wished I hadn't won it at all. Purely because I hated all the attention. All those people coming up to me for the next two months, telling me they thought I was great. I found it so awkward. It was inauthentic – nothing to do with the real me, everything to do with someone else's version. I couldn't wait for everyone to forget about it and leave me alone.

It's why I often find one-off exhibition matches more enjoyable than the big tournaments. I can just pitch up and play. If I'm running twenty minutes late, I can ring them up: sorry, stuck in traffic, won't be long. No worries, Ron, cup of tea's waiting for you, looking forward to seeing you when you get here. In and out in a couple of hours and no hassle when I pop off at the end. I can be me.

There's not many people understand what it's like to be famous. Imagine you're a gardener, and every time you go out, complete strangers come up to you and stop you in the street and say, love what you did with that herbaceous border, can you tell me how to get my lawn looking better? You pop to the shops, except you can't get up and down the aisles because people you've never met before want to show you photos of their window boxes, and then ask you for some free bulbs, and then want a selfie with you where they're doing some strange gardening pose. Except they can't remember how their phone works because they're suddenly all fingers and thumbs, so you have to take it for them, and now everyone in the shop is queuing up for gardening chat and you just want to pay for your bread and milk and tea bags and get home.

I've got a mate who's a doctor. Any time I've been running with him he ends up getting it in the ear from others who knows what he does. The front of my left knee hurts, any idea? I've had a cough and it won't shift, what's your advice?

He's there because he's a runner. He's not working. And seeing him in that position helps me in a way, because it makes me realise that I'm not crazy, not wanting to talk about my job when I'm not doing my job.

I listened to an interview with Cristiano Ronaldo a little while ago. He said he hasn't taken his son to the park in ten years. The one time he tried, the whole place stopped and rushed over to him. He said, they weren't being themselves, I wasn't being myself, and it wasn't good for anybody, so I'll never do it again.

I'm not Cristiano Ronaldo. But I've seen what fame does to people, and I find it deeply uncomfortable. I'm not looking for adulation when I play snooker. I'm looking for satisfaction, and a challenge, and a never-ending puzzle. I love the connection snooker can make between me and other people, but I look at it in a different way.

You know the way some Buddhist monks live that pure life, where they travel about and people look after them and feed them, and the monks aren't out to gain anything but a better understanding of what they're trying to do? That's how I'd love to be with my snooker. My cue brings me closer to real people. It creates a connection which isn't about money and isn't about fame. It's about being with people that are happy to have you around.

People love sport and they love snooker. When you walk into a snooker club to play an exhibition, you see people who can't believe you're there. You're giving them something and they're giving you a welcome in return.

There have been times when I've been at my academy in

Singapore, and there have been seven or eight people there watching me practise, and you can see it's magic to them. To share that with them makes you feel lucky. It makes me feel that wherever I might go in the world, if I turned up at the local snooker hall I would get fed, I would have a place to sleep, I'd be looked after.

I want to have real conversations with people. I want to have real relationships. I don't want people blowing smoke up my arse; I don't want people doing stuff for me that they wouldn't normally do for someone else. I'll instantly know if someone I meet hasn't recognised me, because they talk to me in a normal way, and I can feel myself relaxing with every word we exchange. But it works the other way round too, when you bump into someone dog walking, and it's lovely and normal the first time, and the second time, and then the third time they say, Oh, my mate loves you, could you do him a video message, and your heart sinks and you think, oh, we've messed this up now, haven't we . . .

I try to stay rational about it. If people love the way I play snooker, I'm proud of that. If people have bought into what I do, at least it's legitimate. I've won seven world titles, seven UK Championships, and seven Masters. It's up there with anybody in any field of sport. I don't go looking for attention, and I haven't created it through artificial means. I've never sold a story to the papers to make myself look better; I don't big myself up on Instagram, or pretend things are perfect in a world where they're not. I've written this book to tell the truth, to correct some of the preconceptions and to share some of the things I've learned along the way. This is my life, not the stuff you might hear from someone else.

If you like me, it's because it's all genuine: what happened with my dad going away and my mum going away, me losing the plot and coming back trying to make the best of my career, becoming a snooker purist. I don't see myself as a brand. I'm a real person with flaws, trying to find my own solutions.

I don't feel proud of myself. I'm not showing off. I still see it like we talked about Tiger Woods seeing it: everything a fight, always thinking about the next battle, always plotting how I'm going to get through the next five or ten years. When people say to me, Ronnie, you've done so well, you should be so proud – I don't get any of that. I never look back and think, yeah, I've done great things.

Because it wasn't always like this. There was a day when it all changed. When I went from a snooker player that only people in snooker knew to someone everyone had an opinion about. A day I began as a seventeen-year-old kid and ended as the person getting stopped in the street.

I didn't know it, at the time. I was just playing snooker. The 1993 UK Championships at the Guild Hall in Preston, each day and each round like a tour of my heroes, and an impossible dream.

Beating Ken Doherty in the last sixteen, five years on from staring at him in awe and wonder at Ilford snooker club. Getting past Steve Davis 9-6 in the quarter-finals, still in love with his technique and his style and the sweet sound of his pots.

Against Stephen Hendry in the final. Hendry twenty-four years old and somewhere close to his peak, three world titles behind him, world titles to follow in each of the next three years. Going toe to toe with him, slugging it out with big breaks and big shots. First to ten frames, and stretching it out from 3-2 to 4-2, to 6-2, to 7-2. Him coming charging back, because he's Stephen Hendry, and me wobbling, and holding on, and chipping away, and suddenly at 9-6 and needing just one more. Just one more . . .

UK Championships final, Preston Guild Hall, 28 November 1993

Okay. Me to break. Decent contact off the pack, cue ball back up behind the colours.

Hendry's trying to leave the white safe on the bottom cushion here. Might be a touch short – this red might go to the right corner. Only half a chance, but I fancy this.

Yeah, I've hit that well. Up for the blue – get this, and I can tidy the table up.

Roll it in, up the table a little to take on the red Hendry sent back up playing that safety. This'll go left centre, but there's not many reds available after this, so I'll have to get into the pack soon.

Another blue, cue ball past the pink to pick off a couple of these nice stray reds.

A lick of my lips, chalk on my cue tip.

Bit straight on this black. The position off that red could have been better. I can only go backwards or forwards with the cue ball now.

Black in, screw back off the side cushion.

20 points up, but messy on this next red. Cueing right over the pink, making the game hard work.

Now that is a good red. My touch feels good here. I'm hitting the ball well.

Pink to the bottom left. Back round for a stray red to the same pocket.

This is the shot now. Nice angle on the black to go into the pack. Play this with power . . . yeah, lovely, that's opened them up.

Playing with pace now. Red to the left middle, up for the blue, sink that and get on this next red with the referee John Williams still re-spotting the colour.

41 ahead. Easy red, easy black. 49 ahead.

Four or five reds in pottable positions. Take that one, get on the black. Roll that one into the right middle, pick off the blue again.

Red and a good colour here and he'll need snookers.

Don't think about the money. Don't think about the telly.

Screw back off this red. Punch the black into the right corner.

Sudden burst of applause from the crowd. They know.

71 ahead, 67 left on the table.

Beautiful.

Playing my pace. No doubts in my head.

See the pot, get down over it, sink it.

Get the rest out for a red into the left corner. Bit out of position on this blue, but that red to the right corner will go . . . yep . . . One more black. Into the last three reds around the pink. Not sure any will go here – I'll try that red to the right middle . . . nah, doesn't matter, we're done here . . . Shaking hands with the referee. Hendry coming over. Shaking hands with him.

Look at him. My hero. Does he know? I went out last week and bought the exact same shoes as him, just to be more like him. If he does something, I should do it, right?

Back to my seat. Smile, Ronnie, smile. Let it go . . . All the fans leaning over. I'll shake his hand, and her hand, and his. Bloody hell, they ain't letting go, some of them. And I've got to go get that trophy . . .

It all changed after that, of course. The youngest player ever to win a ranking event, the first time I'd won anything on television. The final all over BBC TV at peak time on a Sunday evening.

So many strange things that night, so much to follow. My mum coming on from somewhere at the end and giving me that many kisses my face still was covered in her lipstick when I was interviewed by BBC presenter David Vine a little later.

Hendry going up to her and offering his congratulations, and her buzzing off that too.

'Stephen Hendry's just shaken my hand!'

I had no idea. I had no expectations. Just playing from love and joy, barely able to believe I was there at all.

Pure snooker, for me. No politics, no nonsense. Pure snooker, for a final few hours.

Some people love what fame does to them. I've seen it happen. And maybe part of me wishes I could be one of those people, spending your whole life on Instagram, showing people you don't know and will never meet everything you're up to, pretending to be the fittest person on the planet when you're not. Pretending you never crack.

I've had really famous people want to be my friend, purely because of what I do. I've usually ignored them. Nice people, but too famous for me.

I find it genuinely scary. Who wants all that attention? Who wants to be out running in the woods and some geezer with a camera pops out from behind a tree? I don't even go out in public much. I do my running early in the morning, in the quiet places. I stay inside for most of the day. If I want to go shopping I go at ten o'clock at night when it's empty.

There's a restaurant nearby that I love going to. Problem is, the main man in there can't help but talk to me for twenty minutes. I'm thinking, you're a lovely guy, but I've come here with Laila in order to talk to Laila. So I get a takeaway now, because I can't take the chance. He doesn't think he's being rude, and he's not – not under usual rules of engagement. Most people I meet are incredibly nice. They're excited to see you, so it's not their fault. But it's never just one person. It's twenty in an hour.

It's the same conversation played on a loop throughout every moment you're out and recognised.

It's not that I'm some kind of saint and those who court celebrity are the sinners. We're just different. I know myself well enough now to realise that if I try to sit in a meditative state and wait for a beam of light to come through the window and fill me with feelgood vibes, it's not going to work. I have to connect properly with other people.

It used to occasionally get me in trouble. I was so insecure in the past I thought everyone else had the answer, whether it was some random at a tournament telling me how I should be cueing, or someone with the supposed secret to healthy eating. I spent a lot of time searching when I was younger. I was open all the time.

I'm still not always brilliant at reaching out. Sometimes I don't like burdening people, because I know they've got their own issues to cope with.

But I'll never make the mistake of not connecting. There are people now I trust with my life, and I feel lucky to know them. About a year ago, coming into Christmas 2021, I suddenly found myself in a bad place, out of nowhere, and all the alarm bells were going off.

This is dangerous, mate. This could go properly wrong. I could do something really stupid. . .

So I sent a few texts. That's usually the way I do it. I'm no good at pretending. I'm a terrible liar; I can't hide a thing.

And it pulled me back from the cliff edge. Friends checking in on me every day, twice a day, three times a day. A mate who lives in Liverpool, phoning me – Ronnie, I'll get in the car, I'll come down and pick you up, come and stay with me for as long as you need. I will get you through it.

John's humour, his positivity, his love, all helped find a light in the darkness. Suffering in silence seldom works in the long run. At some point it's going to come back and bite you on the backside. You don't have to keep talking about it, but you need to get it off your chest. Get it out there. Say, it's done, it's over.

I've got to be honest and I've got to say how it really is for me. I've been caught out once or twice doing something I knew wasn't authentic, and it felt terrible. I'd rather go to live on an island by myself and never have to face anybody else. And so I've learned to set boundaries around myself.

If a kid or an older person asks for a photo, I'll do it. I'll always do autographs. Anyone else and I have to say a polite no. If I'm having dinner with family and friends, I'm not going to accept an invitation to go over to a stranger's table to say hello, or speak to their dad on the phone. When I'm in China – and I love going to China, the food, the culture, the people – I can't say yes to the hundred people waiting for me every morning in the reception of my hotel. I'm not a monkey in a cage. There's only one in a thousand who turns out to be an idiot, but you have to keep something back for yourself, or you'd go mad.

They can be hard for us to establish, boundaries. They don't come naturally to me, and you don't need them in every area of your life. But in certain situations, with certain people, they can be a great tool to have. You can't be everyone's friend, and you can't live your life to the desires and whims of others.

If you're going to try it, start with a few simple ones. A couple of micro-boundaries. Don't be scared of saying it. See how it goes. Once you've done that, you realise you can put others in place.

It might be explaining to a manager that you're not going to answer work emails at weekends. Maybe you start smaller: I'm not going to look at work emails on weekend evenings. But people will adjust to you, and they will respect you more, and you'll be happier.

In China, I worked on my own boundaries. The first morning I came down from my hotel room there were fifty people waiting for me to step out of the lift and fifty more in the lobby. Everyone wanting photos and a chat, and twelve balls signed. So I said to them, today is Wednesday. On Saturday, I'll come out in the morning and I'll sign everything you want. Today, nothing. Thursday and Friday the same. I need to play snooker. But Saturday, we'll get it all done.

It was almost miraculous. They were all absolutely fine with it. On Wednesday, Thursday and Friday, I walked through the hotel, smiled at a few people and got on my way happy. I could enjoy all the things I love about China. Then Saturday came, I set up a table and chair in the lobby, there was a nice orderly line, and everyone got their memorabilia. It worked for all of us. Running has taken me away from the crowds. Establishing boundaries has balanced out the natural people-pleaser in me.

But having boundaries is not the same as cutting yourself off from the world. A friend of mine from rehab said to me once: Ronnie, you're more like a human doing, rather than a human being. He didn't mean it in a complimentary way. He was deep into the Twelve Steps, he was chasing peace. He didn't want any stress in his life in case it took away his well-being.

It's not a bad way to live your life. I loved him for that, the way he'd tried to find a balance that worked for him. I was envious of him, in some ways. But I knew it wouldn't work for me. I've got a family to feed, and anyway, I'm not the sort of person who could be happy smoking roll-ups all day and filling my time with NA meetings.

He was right; I am a human doing. I'm no good at sitting

around doing nothing. I need to be busy, whether that's cooking, or cutting the grass, or painting. I don't feel good when I'm at home sitting on the sofa watching Sky Sports. I feel great when I'm cutting up onions and chicken and making a nice bit of stir-fry. Sometimes I cook not because I want to cook but purely for how good it is for me. I know it's nourishing, and the smell of freshly cooked food makes it feel like a home, not just a hotel room where I have a take-away and sleep and wake up and move from one tournament to the next.

You might have seen that amazing climbing documentary, *The Dawn Wall*. It's about a free climber called Tommy Caldwell who wants to climb a 3,000 ft rock face in Yosemite. He's a natural. Unbelievable talent. But when he's twenty-two, he loses his index finger in an accident, which should be him finished. It's the finger you need to find holds and lock your grip. Instead, he begins to work out a way of carrying on, because he won't give up, and he's too engrossed in his sport, and this is all he has – more than anything else in his life.

Well, that's me and my snooker career. My life. I ballsed it right up. I made a complete mess of it, but gradually I've put it all back together again.

And maybe that's the whole point. Sometimes, if you want to make the grade, you've got to keep being broken. You've got to have the strength of character to keep going back for more. That's how you become unbreakable, in the end.

As I've moved through my thirties and into my forties, each year has become more precious to me. When I was younger I would let them fly past. Sometimes that was even easier.

Don't look too close, you won't like what you see . . .

Now, coming up to fifty, I want each year to be a really good one. And so I am much more open to looking at people and thinking, okay, they've got their life right – what is it I like about how they're doing it?

Never give up learning from other brilliant people. That's the heart of it. Good people can teach us to do something better than we can do it ourselves. People who don't just talk a good game, but live and breathe what they say. The key is to be alert to what it is they're doing so well.

Which brings us back to Steve Peters. I always go back to Steve, because he brought everything to life for me.

Stephen Hendry and Steve Davis were like machines. John Higgins and Neil Robertson and Judd Trump are like robots, in a good way. I'm not. I'm a mad mishmash of emotions and thoughts and ups and downs. That's why I needed help in figuring out a way through.

Steve taught me about challenging the beliefs we have hard-wired into us. From the beliefs come the crippling emotions, and we had a pretty long list of them for me.

Feel good, play good. Feel shit, play shit, lose, go home.

Right. The challenge to that was a simple one: your game might be shit, but your mind can be good.

I can't win if my tip isn't perfect. If my cue doesn't feel exactly right.

Steve would say, I'm not having that. Two years ago your tip wasn't right, and you won the Masters.

Alright, Steve, I'll give you that one.

I can't win a tournament playing badly.

Except you can, Ronnie, because you have. You can play your way into it.

It's still hard for me. I was a sabotage genius. I could sabotage the hell out of any situation, and I still can. It's like a train with no brakes, like a form of self-harm. But I know now it's not

192

right. I know it's not a rational thing to do. You can recognise it, once you get into the habit.

Here's how I'll do it before a game of snooker. I know the chimp will do his best to tell me I'm not good enough. He'll start busy and get louder, and once I'm listening to him, he'll run away with me – I'm not feeling good, I'm past my best, I want to go home . . . Fine. That's just the chimp doing his job, trying to hijack me. So I'm going to do my job. I'll start with a blank piece of paper, with one question at the top: how would I like to feel here? Then I write down my answers. I want to feel focused. Determined. I want to compete. I want to enjoy it. And I want to win, because winning is nice, and we all like to win, we're just not going to be defined by it.

Those are five really beautiful things for me to get out of any match. If the self-sabotage begins, I return to them. Here's how I'm going to be. Here's how I want to feel. And from there the good feelings flow: I do want to be here, I don't want to lose, I am still a good player.

You can use the same technique in any area of your life where you think you're self-sabotaging. Next time you're in a stressful situation, ask yourself the same question: if I could choose, how would I like to feel? Maybe you have to stand up and speak in public, and it's not your natural sweet spot. The chimp will tell you you're going to mess up. You'll fluff your words, you'll forget where you are. Okay. How do you actually want to feel? Confident. Passionate. You want to enjoy it. And you want to finish looking forward to the next time you do it. Here's how you're going to be.

Since connecting with Steve in 2011, I turn round matches I could never previously have turned around. That's why, in the last decade, I have become the ultimate player. There are a lot of strong guys on the table – Higgins, Selby, Williams,

Trump. Hendry was unbelievably strong. The rest are hit and miss. They have their frailties. And that's fine. It's okay to have frailties. But I genuinely think I might be mentally stronger than any other player now.

You know the old-fashioned travelling circus that pitches up in your local park every year? I always loved the hall of mirrors they would have in them. This room where you walked in, and every mirror you looked into gave you a different stretched-out version of yourself.

That's how I see friendship. That's what it's like for me, connecting to other people. Each person you invite into your world naturally brings out a slightly different part of your personality.

Steve Peters is the scientific man in my world. Ronnie, we're going to work this out. Damien Hirst is the feels man. He comes from the artistic perspective. He believes in the spheres, and knowing when they are all aligned. He says that to me a lot.

Sometimes I'll have to say to Steve, mate, this is not happening today. But Damien gets that. He'll say, Ronnie, if you're not feeling it, let's just go home and cook some dinner. I can see you're suffering. I don't want you in here.

He understands what it's like, Damien. He gets the idea of flow. When he's working at what he does, sometimes it just isn't there. And he's good at reminding me that snooker is just a game, and having a laugh and a joke, but he's also a serious guy when it matters. He gets there's a job to be done. Ronnie, we're here to win today, right?

You recognise yourself in other people, when you connect. All of us are hybrids. And when I think about the snooker players I spend time with, I think I'm made like Jimmy White but I've learned to be more Stephen Hendry.

I admire Hendry like you wouldn't believe. When you have a conversation with him there are no ifs and buts. He's so logical. 'This needs doing, I am here to win; I am out, I am not playing.' Like a machine. That's a great way to be as a sportsman. Just put everything in its box.

Jimmy? Jimmy's like a big brother to me. A lot of times people will talk to me about snooker, and I listen and nod and think, you're talking a right load of nonsense. Always full of excuses – 'Oh, I was unlucky,' and this and that. I've heard that story since I was ten years old, and it's never accurate. When I have a chat with Jimmy, it's the opposite. He actually gets it. He's been there and done it.

Jimmy's highs and lows are higher and lower than most people will ever experience in their lives. He still never feels sorry for himself. He's loved his career and he loves his life. You want more of him in your world because he brings out the happy part of you. The part where it's all a mad game. You ever need an excuse to get out of something? Ring Jimmy, because Jimmy has always got a brilliant story.

'Ronnie, just tell them your cue's been broken. You're at the mender's, and you're doing your best, but right now you can't play, and you can't go anywhere because you've got to make sure they do a proper job . . .'

Jimmy's almost done it the wrong way around. Most twenty-year-olds in the 1980s were playing *Space Invaders* in their bedrooms. Jimmy was out in nightclubs with Tony Knowles until three in the morning. I prefer the Jimmy of today: a more stable figure, a great parent to his kids, a doting grandparent. That's the one that brings out a part of me I like.

He can push me too, like Damien.

'Come on, Ron, you've got seven world titles. You got to aim for eight.'

'But Jim, I'm enjoying myself, I don't want to be a slave to the game. It's going to them dark places I don't want to go.'

'But you're the best. Go and seize it.'

'Really?'

Because that's the thing. You don't always see in yourself the things your friends do. Hendry knew what he had. Hendry used to tell his wife before the World Championships had even started: don't forget to bring my dinner suit up for the party after the final. I never had that confidence. So Jimmy puts the wind in my sails. He knows when my tyres need pumping up.

I am a vulnerable person. That's the thing. So I tend to surround myself with people that I feel safe with, and that's what it's like with my mate Robbie.

We met about twelve years ago through a mutual friend. Both of us single at the time, me travelling about to different tournaments and lonely on the road. Robbie started coming along to keep us both company, and I always seemed to do well when he was around. So all this time on, he's still my tournament man. In his late fifties, retired, doesn't need to work, wants to sit back and enjoy life. That's perfect for me.

He balances me out, Robbie. He teaches me some top-notch table manners, or tries to. He's protective when too many people try and climb into my world. And he's not at all about the snooker, which is the big thing.

'Ronnie, you're my mate and I want to see you do well, but if you're not feeling it and you don't want to be here, that's fine as well.'

I couldn't have someone around me at tournaments who was just all about the snooker. I've had that sometimes with coaches and other people, and it burns my head out. I can go and play snooker. Lovely. But I don't want to be talking about it and thinking about it all the time. Robbie knows so little about snooker that if I come back to our hotel room and he says I've played really bad, I know I've actually played really well. If he says I've played really well, I know I've played shocking.

'Robbie, what do you reckon to that?'

'Yeah, you were brilliant.'

'What game have you been watching? That was absolute shit!'

We'll spend twenty weeks a year together at tournaments, and we'll have a great time, and when we're done I drive back to London and he goes back to his wife and family in Manchester. There's no need to text. If he needs me, I'm there; if I need him, he's there.

Then there's Chris. Another different man, another mirror. I've told you how my life started in 2000 when I went to rehab and began having clean and sober friends around me. Chris was a massive part of that. You talk about people that I have learned from – well, I learned so much from Chris. He's the type of friend I would like to be to other friends.

We were both on that journey of trying to get away from our past, get away from the wreckage of what we'd left behind. Both of us having a problem with drinking, both on the Twelve Steps at the time. A lot of it was based around just keeping our sanity. We were grateful for getting away from that rock-bottom, and we could remember vividly what it was like. We would remind each other: as long as we're both clean and sober, we live to fight another day.

We were almost doing it for each other.

'It's just a game of snooker Ron, there's another one next week. We'll go to a meeting this week, you get back to practice, I'll do my work.'

If we won the tournament there was no drinking, no partying. It was back to the hotel room, have a hot chocolate, pack the bags, get a nice breakfast in and off we go.

You talk to Chris and you always come away feeling better. He has this calming way about him. He also has the Irish mentality of getting the job done, no matter what it is. He would punch through walls for you. Fifteen years ago we were on the floor, no money, drinking, in a dark place, hating life. Now we've got jobs, we're clean, we're sober, we're fit, we're healthy. We're grateful.

Here are things I've learned from being connected to all these good people.

I want to be a nice guy. I value being grateful, I value being humble. I'm grateful for what I have.

I value my running, being out in the fresh air. I value cooking and eating well. I value going to work, I value taking time off. I value sharing what I'm passionate about. I value not working for a pay cheque, most of the time.

I value being able to smile when I miss a shot or play badly.

Being connected helps with every one of those. When I was in the Priory doing rehab, one of the head consultants took me aside one afternoon. She said, 'You're the most competitive person we've ever had in here. We've been monitoring your behaviour, and we had Gazza in here, and you go beyond even what he was like. You should learn how to separate your own happiness from your snooker.'

She was absolutely right. If I had a good day at snooker, I was as high as a kite that night. If I had a bad day, I felt like I hated myself. What way is that to live your life?

Two decades on, it's like Steve Peters reminds me: Ronnie, you have friends who will love you no matter what. Whether you play snooker or do something else.

I still have to work on it daily. On staying connected with those close to me, on not pushing people away because I think

I'm having a bad day of snooker. It's not their fault, so why should I take it out on them? All Laila is trying to do sometimes is put a good meal on the table for us. To create a happy home. And I can come home saying, I don't want to eat, I don't want to talk, I don't want to go out. That's not the sort of life for her, so it can't be the sort of life for me.

I'm better now at playing a match and being able to go out to dinner afterwards. Better at leaving my snooker out of my personal life. I can want to be there with the people I'm with, and I can forget about whatever happened on the table earlier in the day. I couldn't do that before.

All from being connected. From creating a raggle-taggle network of friends from different parts of the country and different parts of my life. From being part of something bigger than myself.

A connection which isn't about money and isn't about fame, but about being with people that are happy to have you around. Who reflect back an authentic part of you. Who teach you stuff you could never have taught yourself.

11

WINNING
HOW MUCH DO YOU WANT IT?

I'm in my hotel room, early January. Bit of a bleak old day outside, grey clouds launching rain against the window. People I don't know are down in the foyer, but they know me, and they know this is the hotel where the snooker players are staying, so I'm sort of trapped in here. Can't really go out for a coffee, can't go for a stroll unless I want to be stopped for selfies all the way, and once you've stopped for one the whole town knows about it, and you'll never get away.

So I make this room my home. I Ronnie-fy it.

This is what you'd see if you walked round with me. There's my oranges and bananas on the windowsill, keeping them as fresh as you can in a hotel with the radiators on full blast. Mug of tea on the side table plus a packet of fags, which I'll be trying not to smoke. A load of dried-out old tea bags in the bin underneath, empty smoked salmon packets wedged in as well.

Past the sofa. My mate Robbie relaxing there, a chilled man, glasses and grey hair. Perfect company for this scenario.

My cue case is in the corner. Away from the radiator, away from the window and direct sunlight, if there were any direct sunlight on a day like today. My suit's in the wardrobe, hanging up ready for the match later on. Like my armour, ready to be lifted on for battle.

Over by the kettle – and the kettles are always too small in a hotel room, when you like a cuppa as much as I do – there's my pots of instant porridge, the breakfast of champions, and my packets of Ibuprofen, because my groin's been sore when I've been out running the last couple of weeks.

Quick look round the door into the bathroom. There's all my running kit, hanging up. We can keep the stink in there, we can dry it off for the next morning. Leggings and trainers, T-shirt and long-sleeved top.

Now. Here we go. In the space I've cleared between the bed and sofa, resting on the low coffee table, there are three small canvases. These are my paintings: a new diversion for these days and these conditions. Canvases, paintbrushes, squeezy tubes of acrylic paint. Damien Hirst steered me this way, and I'm borrowing heavily from his style here, going for abstract dots, some small, some bigger like the blooms of strange flowers.

That's life on the road, when you're closer to getting it right than wrong. Finding an escape from all the stuff that feels like it's squashing you down. Balancing out the pressures that'll come on the snooker table later on.

Because when you want to win, all this stuff matters. Later on this evening I'll be playing on instinct at times, in amongst the balls and in my comfort zone. There will be other moments when my head will have to be strong. When the foundations must be solid and the mind clear.

I'm not gifted like Stephen Hendry when it comes to the big pots. I don't think so, anyway. But I realised pretty early on that if I was going to be a winner I had to start nailing those sorts of shots, and you have to build yourself up for them.

I play snooker a little like Roger Federer plays tennis. I like to cruise my way through matches. I don't want to grind it. But when you're up against the top players – whether it's Rafa Nadal and Novak Djokovic, or John Higgins, Judd Trump, Neil Robertson and Mark Selby – I have to be true to the warrior part of me. I have to commit even when I don't feel like it.

I'm going to talk a lot about winning – how you do it, what it does to you, how it is when the snooker gods are displeased and you fall away and lose. And here's the first thing you need to know: when you start winning, and you keep winning, you feel like you can cope with anything the game throws at you. Between 2001 and 2008 I became so accustomed to winning that I actually began to prefer the more pressurised frames to the easy ones at the start of a match. If it went 8-8 I would feel as calm as you like. I could make a break of 70 or 80 as if it were nothing. Play rubbish all match and then play a great final frame.

When you start losing, all that pressure comes piling back in. Now you're twitching and you're scratching. In the 2020–21 season I made five finals, but I wasn't winning them. In the one final I really fancied, I was only 8-7 down, thought I had a chance of winning, and bottled it. The nerves got the better of me because I'd fallen out of the habit.

You can't be two different players in one body. I can't spend most of my time being a fluent player, potting balls, being the Rocket, or whatever they want to call me, and then when it comes to the nitty-gritty start tightening up, playing like someone whose strengths are different to mine. The snooker gods aren't going to appreciate that. If my bow tie and my waistcoat and trousers are my suit of armour, then the way I play is my shield. And you should be carried out on your shield, not on your knees.

You get over a shot and you don't rush it. You don't slash at it. You take your courage and you hold on to it tight. You think, I'm committed to the pot and I'm prepared to lose.

You might beat me but you ain't going to get no weakness out of me . . .

That's how you have to play. In the hotel room with my paintings and cup of tea and damp trainers I'm ordinary Ronnie. Down here on the table, under the lights, I'm Snooker Ronnie. Armour on, no gaps or chinks for anyone to exploit.

Now these things don't come naturally. These are the skills and techniques you build as you go through your career, as you win beautifully and lose painfully and try to work out the margins in between. When I began, I was in awe of Hendry. I didn't feel worthy of playing him; I didn't believe I could compete with him. I had to get through that to stand any chance. You win a few tournaments, a few matches where you wobbled, and all of a sudden you develop your own style, your own belief system, your own way of playing the games.

Because you have to be you, to win. You have to play to your strengths. Don't try to be me, if it's not who you are. Be who you are, commit, and believe. You might fail, but you're going to fail on your terms, and then you can come back stronger.

I have come up against opponents who are infuriating to play. They've beaten me and I've hated it. But in the aftermath, I haven't tried to change who I am, or else they will keep beating me, and I'll keep falling apart.

Okay, you've got the lock on me at the moment, but I've got the code here to unlock you and turn the pressure onto you. Next time we dance, I'm going to make you feel uncomfortable, and once I do, you're going to make mistakes. I will be going pot pot pot, break break break, and I am going to be on you, and let's see how you deal with that . . .

A good attacker always beats a good defender. There's another reason for me to play this way. You dictate, when you attack. Your opponent is forced to re-evaluate their strategy. When I'm playing snooker and they're trying to tie me down and I keep kicking the door open, they get a panic on. They realise all that tucking me up isn't working. It's feeding me. It's making me stronger. I know the psychology and I can see it and I can feel it too. It's a dog sniffing the air.

I've seen it with Serena Williams. I watched the documentary about her and Venus, and I felt an empathy. The way she has had to battle to make it, the way she has things thrown at her; how she gets her motivation from proving those people wrong.

Serena always came out fighting. That's what you have to do, if you want to keep winning, year after year. It doesn't mean you can't have your vulnerabilities and it doesn't mean you won't lose. She talked in the documentary about being beaten in a US Open final having felt all tournament that her game was a mess. I can't serve, I can't run, my backhand's off.

That's what happens when you've been accustomed to being the best. Part of winning is understanding there will be times when you will come unstuck. There are times when you will win tournaments playing what you term badly, and you wonder how the hell it happened, and there are times you will come up short, because the margins between you and the other elites are slim. When I heard Serena speaking about it, I thought, yes, I'm not the only person who has felt it.

Winning changes you as a person. It develops a core of confidence inside you, and a satisfaction in who you are. It changed me, and I've seen it change other players.

They get a tighter team around them. You don't hear so much about what they're doing. They're almost isolated, as if they're in training camp twelve months of the year. If they have a short period off, they come back lean and they come back focused.

You understand now. You see what professionalism means. Not just what you do on the table, but how you live your life away from it. You cancel things. You calm all the background noise down.

Winning lets you zoom in on those narrow margins. You look at some of the newer kids on the block, and you can see they haven't worked it out yet. You think: your career is stuttering along because you're not ticking all the boxes. You say you want to be a winner, but you're not prepared to dig deep enough, and you're not prepared to sacrifice whatever else you want to do outside the sport. You've got to live it and breathe it and you have to love the sport. You have to block out any distractions.

Becoming a habitual winner makes you look at other players in a different light. When you haven't won big, perversely, you think it must be straightforward. It's only just out of reach. When you start to win, you realise how hard it is. You know what it's sucked out of you. To keep winning is of another magnitude again. I understand that the minute I take my foot off the gas, no matter what I've done in the past, there's always someone else ready to take my spot.

You have to work to stay in that place, work at it all the time. The moment the mind wanders, things can go wrong. Maybe that's why it never becomes boring. I used to love keeping a winning run going.

And yet your definition of success is specific to where you are in life and what you have in your slipstream. At this moment, I don't care where I am ranked in the world. Maybe that's because I never feel any pressure to stay at number one when I get there. I just let it happen. I just play. I always feel I have the measure of every other player as long as I tick each box that needs ticking, so I'll take the hand I've been dealt. I'm here for the long haul.

In a weird way I've sometimes enjoyed dropping down the rankings. I knew my performance must have fallen away for that to happen, and so some would be writing me off. It became an enjoyable challenge for me to climb back up again – and then, when I'd done so, I could appreciate another quiet few years.

That's how it was pre-Covid. I had been doing a lot of exhibitions, less match practice. I just wanted to enjoy my snooker, so my performances weren't great. I was still a top ten player, and that was fine, because I knew why. It wasn't as if I was putting everything into it. Then Covid came along and all the exhibitions stopped, and I began to practise with purpose again, and in the period since I've won two world titles in three years. And I feel comfortable in that situation too.

There are tricks you learn, after a while. When you're at that moment in a match and you're ahead and it looks like the win is yours, never start counting down the frames. One more to go, one more to win? It doesn't work. Just keep going, just keep going. Everything becomes about pushing beyond the finish line. There is no end.

You want a boxing analogy? You don't aim to punch your opponent on the chin. You punch through their chin. Something else I had to learn from boxing: you aim to destroy your opponent, not give them another chance. It's like Mike Tyson told us: 'Every shot was thrown with bad intentions. I was hoping he would get up so I could hit him again and keep him down.'

Hendry helped teach me that, like he taught me so much else. It was the European Open in Antwerp in December 1993. I was seventeen years old; he was the reigning world champion, the best player in the world, but I fancied it, because less than a month before, I'd beaten him in the final of the UK Championship, and it was being hailed as a changing of the guard.

I didn't believe any of that nonsense, but I knew I was playing well, and at 5-4 up in Antwerp I thought I had him again. That's when I put a pink safe on a cushion rather than risking a tricky pot to continue my break.

I thought it was the right move. I thought it gave me a little bit of insurance. So innocent.

Bang! He got in, potted the pink, cleared up and won the next five frames. One little negative shot, played on one occasion, and I was toast. I walked away that night in a daze.

What the hell just happened there? That's how you win the tournament, that's what just happened.

There were times after that where I would feel like I'd fallen across the line. I'd win the tournament, but I didn't feel like a winner. I came off thinking, He missed a ball and let me in. I didn't win it, he lost it.

Hendry and Tyson were still haunting me, and rightly so. It's not the same as coming out all guns blazing from the first frame. Big finals are long matches. You can keep purring along, right up to the moment when you need to punch through their chin. You sense the time is right, and you summon the bad intentions.

It might be the second session of a three-session match, and you're four-all, and you raise it and end that session 11-5 up, job done. It might be the final session, as when I played Neil Robertson in the quarter-finals of the Worlds in 2012. He was the best player in the world at the time, I was ranked 13. I hadn't had a great season, but I'd been working with Steve Peters and I knew my game was good. 11-8 up, and I realised this was the time.

I've got to come out with some bombs here. I've got to play winning snooker.

I had a shot to nothing on a red at the start of the twentieth frame. Very missable. White close to the baulk, red eight feet away down the table and still two feet from the left corner pocket.

I took it on.

Normally you'd pot it, if you were playing really well, then aim to come round the back of the black and play for a baulk colour. Sometimes the white goes behind a baulk colour and you snooker them. Sensible snooker.

Instead, I hit it so hard. Absolutely smashed it. Rather than coming off two cushions, I came off one, two, three, four cushions, in and out of baulk. All the way round the table and back again. Four cushions!

That is beautiful. Lovely . . .

I've never seen anyone play it like that. So confident in my cueing I had total control over how I was hitting the ball. I thought, There's a good chance I'm going to win the World Championship now. It's hard to compete with this.

I ended up beating Robertson 13-10. I'd done to him what Hendry did to me. I knew that, even if I wasn't feeling super confident, I had to go out there and play as if I was. And doing that made you feel good. It made you confident. In that final session that night I was making 100s, I was making 90s. I knew I had it.

Even if I miss a pot and let you in, you're going to leave me half a chance, and I am going to nail it.

I remember, as I walked round the table in the final frame, hearing Steve Davis doing commentary on BBC television. He said, the tournament's done. Only the quarter-finals but he knew, the way I played. That was the way to play. That was the skill I'd learned.

2012 was the year I was at my peak, looking back. I played

probably my best snooker ever; I felt great physically and mentally. And even then, there were the moments in the final against Ali Carter when I started thinking it was my match to lose, when the temptation was suddenly to start playing defensively, to pretend to be a player I'm not.

It would have been suicidal. I had to forget the occasion, forget who I was playing. Forget I had only a couple of frames to win.

And so, it became like meditation. Almost like being in a hypnotic state. Before you know it, your flow comes and you think, whoa, I am now in a pure state in the most tense situation possible.

Then you feel like a winner. Then, you can do . . . anything.

World Championship final v Ali Carter, Sheffield. First session, Sunday, 6 May 2012

I'm in bits here. Food poisoning overnight, throwing up all morning.

Maybe Ali knows, maybe he doesn't. Three frames apiece, slugging it out, waiting for a moment to strike. To change the tempo.

I looked pale when I saw myself in the dressing room mirror before coming out. As white as my shirt. Hair pushed back from my face, eyes hollow and watery.

The balls are all over the place. The blue's the only one on its spot. The black is tied up with some reds on the bottom cushion, the pink is nudging a red on the right side, the brown and the green up tight to the baulk cushion.

The reds are everywhere. Four on the bottom cushion, three on the right, two up the other end of the table.

I've been missing. Three reds in a row. But now Ali's missed a straightforward red to the left centre, and I've got another chance, although with the balls like this I might make 20, maybe 30.

Stun the first red in. Top left pocket. A real horrible green here, potting into a blind pocket, but I'm cueing well, so I fancy it.

Nice. Using the far jaw, and when you start hitting it there, you're hitting to the wide part of the pocket, and that's when you know you're cueing well.

I want to tidy this table up. I'm looking at it now and it's a mess. We need to get the balls back into place so it starts looking like a snooker table again.

Brown slides in. I'll have to work in blocks here, in areas. Clean this part of the table up, then move to the next one. Not going directly for position on the next shot, but using the cushions, drifting the white into the middle of the table to give me more area to play with.

Red, blue to left centre.

I want to get the black and the red out here. I could slam into them. But you know what, I've got options here. I fancy I'm going to get the right side of the blue. I fancy I'm going to get the right side of the red.

44 ahead. A tight red along the bottom cushion, not a natural angle on it to take me back up for the blue, so I'll have to bounce it in a bit, get the distance on the white.

White drifting towards the right middle pocket. Don't go in, don't go in . . . Off the knuckle, stays up.

I'm still fucked. It's done. There ain't no way this break is continuing.

Long brown to the top left pocket. Cue ball off the baulk cushion, the left side, the right side, all the way down to pick off another red.

That was pinpoint position. And that one there, another nice red, nice bit of side and again, right side of the blue.

I don't need the black no more. I'm 49 in front, I just need one more red. I'm not going into the black, I'm gonna come off the cushion after the blue, disturb these three balls on the right here – two reds, the pink. Don't know which red I'm going to hit, but I do know I'm going to get into that cushion deep enough to make sure I get a solid contact on the red.

Make it.

Bit of a smelly red, this one. It'll just about go past the pink into the right corner, and it's a bit like the green at the start of this break, into a blind pocket, but the way I'm cueing it, I fancy I'm going to hit the wide part of the pocket.

Tough shot but I'm not worried about this. Nice pause on the backswing, good delivery . . . Bang. Game over.

Clearance will be a bonus now. Chalk out of me pocket, onto my cue tip.

Long red, everything straight in a line, bosh. Lovely noise as it goes in.

Now this brown is ridiculous. On its spot, the white to the left of the pink spot, but the way I'm feeling now the pockets look massive and the balls are small.

I can't miss. I feel like I'm playing on a pool table.

I don't miss.

So here I've got the line, deep into that cushion, perfect cannon on the red and black on the bottom cushion. The white is travelling a lot but I'm totally confident I'm going to get there.

Black into a blind pocket. In off the far jaw, it's not even knuckled. Seeing it really well now.

Fucking hell, mate, this is a break now!

These shots are like body blows to Ali. It's hard to take when you see someone doing this. He understands all them little miracles I'm putting together.

Every shot the crowd are oohing and ahhing. I had this with Hendry. He'd do stuff like this and you'd think the crowd was laughing at you. Laughing at what he's just done. You feel a little bit humiliated. You feel embarrassed.

Last red, little bit of an angle on the black. Perfect.

My white is always in the middle of the table. Always near the next ball, always drifting into it. I'm not playing into a spot, I'm playing for a line. As long as I am close to that next ball, I'm in.

Brown goes in, blue follows.

I ain't missing this pink. I'll have to switch and play it left-handed, but that's no dramas.

In you go. Straight on the black and in.

That is probably as good a break as you will ever see.

Only 4-3, first session, but all the issues are Ali's now. A lot of players would roll over now. One thing he can do is compete. He's a fighter.

But I'm picking the battles. I'm feeling alright.

Sick? I'll be okay . . .

It's never personal for me, beating someone. I don't fixate on them as a person.

When I was a kid and I had no damage to my play, when I felt technically great, it was about dominating. Not winning all the time, but owning the table. Being out there on my own.

Had I not gone through that seven years up to 2000 when I destroyed my game, maybe it would have been more personal. Experiencing that hell made me want to win again for different reasons. I thought I was going to spend the rest of my career like that. It's why I took drugs, it's why I capitulated. I just couldn't cope. I just couldn't accept it.

The worst thing was watching other players doing what I wanted to do and what I used to do. I thought I couldn't even compete with them. Watching John Higgins and Mark Williams – not just their big wins, but the way they were playing.

The reason why they were winning was the way they were going about their business. The way they hit the ball, the way they delivered the cue, their technique, their set-up. I'd play them and it was horribly obvious to me.

This so-and-so ain't going to miss.

Over nineteen frames, what they were doing was sustainable, and what I was doing wasn't sustainable. There was no purring along for me, and that was mentally tough to take. I either had to do something about it or carry on as I was, which was drinking, taking drugs, losing the plot and seriously considering giving up.

What pulled me back from the edge was realising I didn't want a life looking at somebody else wishing I was them. I wasn't prepared to live with that. Winning was a secondary concern, almost a by-product. I just wanted to get back to a place where I fancied getting my cue out of its case and could actually enjoy playing.

I wanted to win my first world title. Once I'd done that in 2001, the pressure was off. I didn't feel the compulsion to win. I was just happy I had my love back for the game.

The noise of the ball hitting the back of the pocket, the noise of the tip hitting the cue ball, that snap, that feeling. That's what I play for now. Enjoying the competition, enjoying the practice, not dreading playing. And I'm incredibly grateful, because there was a long stage in my career where I thought, *I am never, ever going to experience what I felt as a kid playing this game.*

I want to play my snooker like peak Pep Guardiola's Barcelona. I want to play like Messi. That means playing with feel, with flair. It means touch so subtle it can't be taught.

It also means having the structure in your game to make it work. Messi was the greatest player in the world in that Barca team because he understood the framework he was playing within. He allowed Pep to coach him, to improve the aspects of his game you can't see yourself when you're in the middle of it all.

That's what I have to do too. I need coaching, I need solid technique. I'm instinct but I'm science as well. As a mate of mine said, you need scaffolding in place before you can build a beautiful house. To put it another way, Jimi Hendrix could play those insane note-bending solos because he understood scales and arpeggios and chord progressions. All the creative arts are about discipline before they're about anything else. There's a right way and there's a wrong way and you have to do it the right way.

At some point in every season, I will need help. I can't self-teach, any more than Barcelona could succeed without a manager. Even with someone like Messi, there's always a coach who can add to their game. You have to keep listening, even at the top. You have to be open-minded to keep winning.

I've told you about that run I had in 2020–21 when I kept making finals and not winning them. For the preceding months I had been working with a new coach, and I liked what he was adding to my game. He gave me a solidity. He slowed me down; there was a lot of standing behind a shot, checking, holding the cue, walking in. He made me much more methodical and reliable.

I made heaps of semi-finals. I made all those finals on top. I was playing great and feeling good. At the same time, I kept coming up short against certain players.

Only at the end of the season did I work it out: I needed to balance all that with some of my old spontaneity. I'd lost my burst of pace, the fear I'd been able to generate in opponents where they suddenly think, blimey, this match could be over in five minutes.

I wasn't blasting players away anymore, like Hendry had shown me, like I'd done against Robertson and Carter in 2012. I knew it was holding me back. And I thought, I would rather play mediocre for six tournaments but play really great for six more. I don't want to play steady for twelve tournaments. I want to win or go out in the quarters. I don't want semi-final, final, final, runner-up, runner-up. That's no good to me.

It took me eighteen months to get it right. To marry it up with flow, with instinct. To find more compression and down-force in my cueing and get my arm working like a piston, and to cut loose with bad intentions too. To keep the best parts of the technique but to find the right balance between science and style.

Without that instinctiveness I wouldn't have beaten Judd Trump in the World Championship final in 2022. I wouldn't have beaten Higgins in the semi-final. I wouldn't have scared them enough. I'd have been too ploddy to get over the line.

Life is always richer and more rewarding when you stay open to unusual influences as well as the obvious ones. I've been listening to a podcast from an endurance exercise expert called Dr Stephen Seiler. He talks a lot about learning to peak for certain races, about limiting the amount of pressurised situations you put yourself in. I've taken that philosophy from running and brought it into my snooker, because I've tried going hard in every tournament and winning every one, and it's exhausting. You don't even win the ones you want to win because you've given too much trying to win the smaller ones that don't matter as much.

Gary Lineker used to refuse to take shots at goal during his warm-up when he was a player, apparently because he felt it used his goals up when it didn't matter. Well, I was using all my wins up. And it was high risk, in some ways; I couldn't sacrifice the smaller tournaments to just do okay at the biggies. But I had to do it. I want to win the World Championships, the Masters, the UK Championships. There's no point winning the two events before each one because I am not going to be at 100 per cent when it matters.

Something else that may sound strange. Maybe contradictory too, considering what else I've said. Even if you can keep winning, and winning, it becomes boring. I had a ridiculous run in 2017–18. I beat Kyren Wilson to win the English Open, I beat Judd Trump to win the Shanghai Masters. UK Championships, won against Shaun Murphy. Same with Ding Junhui at the World Grand Prix, then Murphy again at the Players Championship.

All that from October to March. And by the end of that run, I was sick. Depressed as hell. I'd pick up a trophy, go back to my room and get pissed and caned with my mate in a daft attempt to get some pleasure from something that felt so flat.

I couldn't work out why I wasn't enjoying it. The strangest of sensations: trophy, cheque, get me the hell out of here. I won the UK Championship, the second most important tournament in my life, and I hated it. It got so bad I was even sick of getting my suit on. Didn't even need to pick up my cue. A glance at a bow tie was enough to make me want to quit.

You might think this makes me a bit weird. We all know about the sporting greats who are defined by how often they win. You think about Tiger Woods and his mad record of going into the final day of a major with at least a share of the lead on fifteen occasions, and going on to win fourteen of them. You think about his winning percentage on the PGA Tour – more than twice as good as any other golfer in history.

There's plenty that does make me weird, but there's logic to this one. Tiger's reputation put fear into every other player.

He also targeted the majors. He didn't try to play or win every event on the tour. And, even at his best, that untouchable winning percentage was around 23 per cent. Extraordinary yes, but still only the equivalent of coming away victorious in a quarter of the events he entered.

In track and field you have the Olympics and the World Championships. The Grand Prix, the Diamond League? The big names put those second. Usain Bolt won three successive Olympic 100 metre and 200 metre golds in part because he peaked for each one.

You have to feel excited when you compete. You have to enjoy the process. You can't just hit a ball. The reason I ended up hating it in 2017–18 was because I had done too much. If you have a prize racehorse you don't race it every weekend. You'd knacker it.

That's what I was doing. I was racing every week, and it crippled me. I didn't hate the game, although there were times when I thought I did. I had lost the excitement and lost the enjoyment.

Self-awareness. Possibly the greatest gift a serial winner can have. I look at Novak Djokovic, and he's so in tune with himself: his diet, his training, his recovery. And when you become aware of your body and mind, it's like you've found the cheat code to keep you going when others would falter.

It was never the game that I hated. The game is a beautiful thing. I was just doing too much of it. It's like I said before: sometimes you have to let it come to you, rather than smothering it with obsessive love.

Never fear defeat. That's the other great insight I've learned. Sometimes a few losses can make you hungry again. Sometimes they can be more enjoyable than a win.

I had a run of playing Judd Trump in the final of the Northern

Ireland Open: 2018 and 2019 at the Waterford Hall in Belfast, 2020 in the Covid time at Milton Keynes. He kept beating me, which made sense; he was number one in the world, he was bang on it. In the first final, I just didn't compete. Didn't give it a crack, and I didn't like it. So the next two finals I had a go. I was super aggressive. I didn't care about the win. If you beat me 9-0, okay. But I'm going to play a game today that is expressive and open.

The way you're supposed to play Judd is to be careful, keep him tight. He's a dangerous player. He's a weapon. As good as they come.

I thought, bollocks to that. He's in form, he always pots well. I can't out-power him. The only thing I can do here is, when I'm in the balls, make sure I create stuff. Judd is, pot ball, split them open, clear up. Me? I pick them off, play some nice positional shots, take three reds out. Bump, bump, bump.

In the 2020 final I was aggressive from the first shot.

Ronnie, there's no feeling your way into this game.

He went 2-0 up early on.

Got to stay aggressive here. Come on, snooker gods. Give me half a chance, I'm ready to score . . .

And I matched him. A proper ding-dong. Big scoring – century breaks, 90s, 80s. He won 9-7, but I came off thinking, cor, I really enjoyed that. The pleasure of the contest outweighed the buzz a victory would have brought.

I know the clichés of elite performance. Once you're happy losing, you're done for. You've got to hate it. Keep the hunger.

Well, it's not true.

Steve Davis taught me a great lesson a few years back. He talked about biorhythms. You are going to have short-term ups and downs. You will also be a different player, a different man, at various times in your life.

Over your lifetime, just as over a thirty-year career like mine, you are going to have bad years. You will also lose your edge at some point. That's fine. It's natural.

Steve taught me to zoom out on the graph. Not to obsess over the small peaks and troughs. To think about the overall picture.

One bad week in your year won't destroy you. One defeat in a season doesn't matter to me. Losing to Judd in Belfast might actually have given me another six years on my career. It showed me the way I should play through the next biorhythm.

I came off that table and that defeat feeling like I had competed. That's all you can do: compete. And if I have competed, there is another tournament next week, and I'll see you there.

That's my greatest asset. I crack, but I don't break. I keep coming back.

12

OBSESSION
BAD DAY, GOOD DAY

I often think that if I just spent my whole life in a snooker club and that's all I'd ever done, I'd be alright.

Years ago, before all this ever looked like it could be a career, I'd go down the club even when I wasn't playing. I'd meet the lads, have a cup of tea, have breakfast. Mess about for a few frames, have a sandwich. Play some kalooki, thirteen-card rummy.

It was like my second home as a young boy, Ilford snooker club. The regulars were my extended family. Down there at the age of ten, and a lad called Simon Thomas always greeting me the same way:

'Alright, you little shit?'

It was easy, when I was a kid. Playing, swearing, winning, playing again. In the game for the love of the game, winning a hundred quid here, five hundred there. All of it like a dream.

Ayrton Senna always said the best days of his life came go-karting as a kid. He called it pure racing. It was pure as a kid for me too: no girlfriends, no hangers-on, no bills to pay. The old snooker halls were like a social club and creche and pub all rolled into one. Rectangles of bright light over the tables, shadows all around. Fruit machines glowing in the corner. So many different characters, old odds and sods coming together under one low roof.

I used to like a game of football too. Trouble was, it would be over too quick, done and dusted in two hours. That included being picked up from home, taken there and driving back afterwards. At the snooker hall I could play a few frames, go on the fruities, have my lunch, play cards, play some more snooker, and then have my tea. I could spend my whole day there.

There were things about that environment I understood and parts I didn't, and sometimes I liked the mysteries even more. So many drinks the adults could choose from. So many different brands of cigarettes. When you grew up it looked like you could never be bored. It looked like everything you could ever imagine was right there for you.

I'm not sure my natural temperament was right for snooker. I always was emotional. Maybe I would have been better off sticking to football. The team-mates to hang about with, the argy-bargy to release the tension. A good old run-around.

But there was something irresistible about it too. I remember walking into the snooker room at the Pontins holiday camp we used to go to, and the whole place would just be . . . *humming*.

All these people, watching, talking, gambling, playing.

You couldn't help but be excited by it all. There was a certain classiness that took it beyond a pub. Men in smart clothes. All these rules everyone adhered to. The neatness of the tables, the way the game involved tidying everything up, putting the mess away in the pockets. People playing billiards, like time had reversed and it was a century ago. Good amateur players on the way up, solid pros with a certain calm power about them.

I could play and be happy. I could sit there watching and feel just as good. Absorbing it all, learning how to behave, how to get away with stuff.

I call it my church, the club I go to now in Walthamstow. Only fifty members, and two tables, and everything looked after properly. It's got the feeling of an old-time billiard hall. Heaps of tradition.

When I'm up the club, I see my mate Mickey and I see the boys. You have a chat, a cup of tea, a bit of this and that. They're playing, they're watching me play. I can see they're happy to have me in the place because they love snooker, and I love being there because I play better when I know someone who cares is watching.

But I'm older now. February 2023, two months into my forty-eighth year. I have battle scars. The purity can get polluted when you stay in this game this long.

There is a fickleness in much that I do. I will have days when I'm up, and the world feels like mine to conquer. Days when I feel my mind is invincible. When I get pissed off with people referring to me as a great natural talent, as if it's an insult, like they're underplaying how much hard work I put in, how strong my character can be.

When I'm up, I think anything is possible. I forget about my limitations. I feel this wonderful force of energy and belief inside me. I feel like Braveheart. Like I'm prepared to die in battle. Like there are no boundaries to what I can do.

Then there are the down days. Except you don't experience them as a bad day, when it's happening. It all seems real and permanent. It seems logical and it feels like now and forever more.

It happened to me again recently. I'd been playing alright in practice; I'd been feeling great. Then, in a first-round match in one of the smaller tournaments on tour, I got found out. Beaten badly, by someone who shouldn't be beating me.

And from there the descent begins.

I think I'm done. I'm done with snooker.

The first thought, swirling round my head. I play below where I know I can play, and all of it is going to come out.

I was feeling vulnerable. Tournaments have usually been the safe space for me; they're where all the hours of practice make sense. This time felt different. I woke up in my hotel room and I didn't want to go out to play. I didn't even want to be there.

I'm forty-seven years old, not twenty-one. This can't go on forever. What if the magic has gone?

The spiral accelerates. A snooker-specific panic attack.

I still love the game, I will always love the game. But I can't just dip in and out. I'm too old, and there's too many hungry young players around for me to have that luxury anymore. I'm not stupid. I know how good the others are.

The next escalation.

I don't want to be on the road, living out of a suitcase.

Thoughts running away from you.

Maybe the World Championships in 2022 was my last big push . . .

I couldn't stop thinking about the bloke who had beaten me. He's okay, as a player. But I could see how badly he wanted to win, and I didn't. I had no patience. I watched him and thought, hurry up, mate, either win it or give me a chance and let me in.

It scares you, when you feel like this. When it feels as all-consuming.

It might be evident by now that I lack confidence, deep down. I always responded best in fight mode. In these dark moments, I don't feel like the switch is there to get angry enough, to get frustrated, to get pissed off enough.

I start to wonder what it would be like if I stopped. What

would everyone say? Would I miss any of it? The competition has always been what's driven me on. I'm not a making-up-the-numbers type of player. So if that goes, why am I doing it?

Beat me, put me out of my misery. I just want to go home.

Snooker always seemed so glamorous. Even now, the World Championships, the Masters and the UK Championships make me feel like that kid at Ilford again. The venue packed out, an atmosphere that makes you want to perform. I remember the days when I would be playing at Goffs Theatre in Kildare in front of sixteen hundred people, and the Irish are always the most passionate snooker watchers. I remember playing in Newport, the Welsh fans taking every seat in every session. The Assembly Rooms in Derby, a thousand more. The Hexagon in Reading: a thousand people in.

After I went out in the first round of that tournament, I couldn't even watch the later rounds on TV. It reminded me too much of the night I was there: a hundred people in the crowd, empty seats everywhere you looked, two blokes having a kip. I could have been playing a pro-am in some social club.

The brilliant players excite you. You play one shot and you immediately know what shot they are going to play, and they know what shot you are going to play next. It's a formal dance. It's chess with spherical pieces. It's an intellectual challenge and it's an adrenaline rush.

You get beaten by an average player, and it feels like a waste of your time. He's got nothing to lose, everything to gain. He'll play all sorts of weird shots. He'll probably get beaten in the next round, because he's achieved everything he wanted already. You find yourself staring into a future that leaves you cold: going through the rest of your career playing nice people who are going nowhere.

We all watched Chicago Bulls superstar Michael Jordan in

the documentary *The Last Dance*. We saw how he motivated himself by starting feuds. By seeing insults where there were none. He needed to be at war with the world to keep going.

I understand it all. When you're fighting to stay on top of the pile you pick something out and decide: This will get me out of bed in the morning, make me fitter and stronger, make me put all the hard work in.

Except what if there are others who want it more? I'm coming up against young players with unbelievable talent. I am playing against fourteen-year-old Ronnie O'Sullivans. I know they're hungry; I can see it in their eyes. I look at them and think: that kid is going to stay here all night if he has to. Ten hours a day he's watching videos of his opponents on YouTube. He's eating his own packed lunch so he can spend more time on the practice table and less time going out for dinner.

It's not the number of titles you win that takes away your desire. It's how much of yourself you have to give to get them.

One morning you wake up and ask yourself: where does this all end?

Hong Kong Masters, Hong Kong Coliseum, October 2022

A better day. A better place.

I've never experienced a crowd like this before. No one has. There's more than 9,000 punters in here tonight, a world record for a game of snooker, and they're responding to every shot we're playing – oohs as a pot rolls towards the pocket, gasps as a ball rattles in the jaws, frantic applause and whooping when the cue ball comes off two cushions and then three and keeps gently rotating to the exact point on the table you want to make the next pot, the next addition to the break.

I'm the man in black here. Waistcoat, shirt, trousers, shoes, bow tie. Darkness all around the arena except the bright rectangle of light around the table.

I've been playing well. 4-1 up in this final against Marco Fu, then 5-2, and then he's come battling back, nicking a couple of tight ones to bring it back to 5-4.

I need one frame for the title, he needs two. And the crowd are sort of torn here, because they adore their home-town hero, but I get proper love here too. They love snooker on top of all that – they know what they're watching, they understand what me and Marco are laying out for them.

We're in the safeties, start of the frame. Marco's clipped the side of the pack, and he's got the white back up to baulk, but one of the reds planted, and has come up just over the left corner pocket.

Easy pot for me, coming off the side cushion to kiss it in, but I've hit the black rather than come round it, and it's gone safe, an inch or two above the centre-left pocket.

Completely out the game. The pink's not really available either, protected by a couple of adjacent reds.

Right. We'll have to plot this one. Blue's free, blue's my ball. Which means it's all about cue ball control. Every red I pot I'll have to get just past the blue, to get the angle to come back down the table for the next red.

Blue to right middle, red to left middle, blue to the same pocket.

Don't really want to smash the rest of the reds open yet. It's too risky, at this point, in this kind of match.

Pick that easy one off the bunch, back up for the blue.

Fucked up. Bit short on it. I'll have to go up the other way.

Blue into left middle. White up the table, between the yellow and brown, off the baulk cushion, off the left-side cushion, all the way down the length of the table and into the meat of the reds.

Applause from the crowd. That's a good shot, that. More reds available now, so let's keep ticking them off, keep getting the cue ball just past the blue.

Forget the black. Don't worry about the pink.

Blues will do me, loads of blues. I'd rather be too long for the blue and on a baulk colour rather than come short on the blue.

Here we go. Green is easier here, have that, back down the table for more of these reds.

Up to 46 points now, Marco watching on.

Red to the left corner pocket. I'll need to screw back here, only a small gap to sneak through between two other reds . . . Great shot. Didn't fancy that one, but thought I had to play it.

Crowd loved that one, I've done a magic trick they never saw coming.

This is all about cue ball control now.

Right side of the blue every time. A sixth blue, a seventh blue. Eight and nine.

Gentle nudge onto the pink off that pot, just to disturb the two reds next to it, open them up.

A tenth blue, up to the baulk cushion, back down. Red, eleventh blue. Red plant into the corner, always going.

The game is over now. I know it, Marco knows it, the crowd know it.

Pink goes to the left middle now. I've hit that really solid, a heavy white, a proper thud. Means I can be more aggressive with it, bring the white right down to the bottom cushion for the final red.

Perfect pace on that. If I'd gone tippy-tappy on that, it'd come up short, but it's rolling on, and on . . . Pinpoint. So much noise in this place!

I'm excited now, proper excited. Looks a simple shot, but it ain't. When you play it well, you just make it look easy.

Going through the colours. Nice angle on the brown, cue ball on

*line for the black . . . tiniest little kiss, nudging it off the cushion
. . . right over the pocket.*

Fucking loving this.

*Blue – easy. Pink goes right corner. Black to left middle – keep
an eye on the white, easy now, don't drop it in the right middle
. . . Done it.*

A total clearance. 114.

*All smiles now. I felt so rusty coming into this, but I love this
place, love the promoters. Had to try my bollocks off.*

Love this game. I love it.

Here's something else I think about when I talk about being
unbreakable. It's understanding that emotions can be fickle.
Once you recognise that, at least you know what's going on,
rather than being confused.

There will be times I play when I'm not enjoying it. There
are tournaments where I'll be playing in front of fifty or a hundred people. The week after I'll be at Brentwood leisure centre
playing in front of twenty-five or thirty, putting my suit in my
rucksack, pulling it out twenty minutes before I play.

It's perversely hard against lower-ranked players when there's
no atmosphere. To stay interested I try to dismantle them
quickly, beat them 4-0 in forty minutes. But you've got to be
playing well to do that, and when I'm not playing well, I don't
want to be there, and that's when they beat me. I start the
downward spiral. I begin to self-sabotage.

Sabotage is being in that match and not enjoying it. Sabotage
is going from not enjoying it to straight away deciding you don't
want to be there. Sabotage is not trying as hard as you could.

When you understand it's just a bad day, and that tomorrow
may well be completely different, it sets you free. The world is
not ending; your emotions are just crowding in on you.

When I've sabotaged, and fallen out of a match I could have won, I've often got back to my hotel room, had a cup of tea, chatted to a mate, and my head has cleared. Now it's more about regret. You realise you might have been able to hang in there. Instead of being out 7-1, it could have been 5-3. You could be in a battle and relishing it again.

We all get stuck in the treacle. We can't get out of the mess we've walked into. It's only later that the logic returns.

This isn't as bad as I thought . . .

Sometimes I'll try to imagine I'm in a helicopter, looking down at myself. Another Steve Peters trick. I zoom out and look at everything around me. I feel small, and less significant, and safer. It matters less, the little moment I'm in.

There will be days when I am trying to find reasons to play, trying to find reasons I want to win. That's what I remember, when I zoom out.

Sometimes, it's really simple. A physical thing.

They used to tell us in the AA meetings: the bad places to be are hungry, angry, lonely and tired. That's when the demons come tapping on your shoulder, taking your hand and leading you astray.

So I try to eat well. I will always try to sleep. I'm not nice when I'm tired; I'm grumpy and snappy. I feel it coming on, and I think, Don't say nothing, Ronnie, it's not fair on those around you. Get your head down for twenty minutes and you'll be alright. You'll wake up in a happier world.

I will kip anywhere. I don't even need to put my feet up. I was doing my punditry for Eurosport at one venue and there was nowhere to sit. The others there were eating bags of crisps, bars of chocolate, necking cans of Coke. I thought, this place is like Sin City. I can't be living like this. I was straight on to Amazon on my phone. Got a £50 bed delivered, set it up in the corner and lay there, chilling out, watching telly, ready to go. I can see the sort of matches that spark the old fire inside. The ones against John Higgins, and Mark Williams. The contests when you'll need to use everything you have – all your talent, and experience, and tricks – just to be competitive. When Williams plays Higgins, I fancy Mark's going to beat him every time; when I play Williams, I generally come out on top. Williams beats Higgins, Higgins beats me, and I beat Williams. Why wouldn't that scenario bring out the competitor in you?

I can see the scenarios that will bring out the fighter in me. That will force me off the ropes.

At the start of 2009 I was in freefall. For two years I couldn't pot a ball. Had one other player lost a certain match I would have dropped outside the top 16 in the world and been forced to go through qualifying for the World Championship. You could hear it again from the gossips and the doubters.

He's going to drop out here, Ronnie. He's done . . .

The bloke won his match. I entered the Worlds ranked 13, thank you very much. And all the stuff I'd heard stuck in my head. It was all I needed.

You fucking wait.

The drive it gave me was irresistible. To win the Worlds in later years from there was a fantastic feeling. Afterwards, I let them know what was inside me.

I will tell you when I am done, but don't anyone ever write me off. None of you are good enough to knock me off my perch just yet.

I have to find reasons to keep playing that make sense to me. Personal ones, things that reflect how I feel. Your drivers might be different. I play so I can financially support my immediate family, because that's something I have to do and want to do. An important enough motivation even if you have nothing else.

I do it to help my running club out. They operate off sub-scriptions, and anyone who's been down a running club will tell you how tight things are for all of them – for keeping the clubhouse going, even if it's only a couple of Portakabins, for paying the electricity bills, keeping the showers working. I like to contribute to all of that in the way I can, and I want them to know that if I were to drop down tomorrow, there is something in my will to make sure a club that's been going for a hundred years can keep operating through this century as well. Running has done so much for me; Ilford Athletic Club gives so much more to the local community.

Good days, and bad days, and you can't let either derail you. I've talked about my iPhone diary notes. Here's the one titled '2022–23 season, 13 events'.

The first entry reads: 'Leicester, 3 games.' Smiley face.

Next one. 'British Open. 1 game. Flat, no crowd.' Bored face.

'Hong Kong. 3 games.' Big smiley face, pure happiness.

'Champion of Champions.' You'd expect a smiley one here. Big tournament, and I won it. Instead, it's a neutral one, and the note underneath explains why.

'Couldn't run. Made me feel down.'

'UK. 3 matches. Flat.'

'Scottish. 3 matches.' Happy face.

'English.' Smiley face. 'Enjoying it again.'

It's taken me half a lifetime to understand, but enjoyment can mean learning to lose. Happiness has to come from every part of my day, not just the snooker.

In 2017 I should have been the happiest player in the world. I'd won the UK Championship, the Shanghai Masters, the Irish Open, I'd won the Champion of Champions. I'd won everything, and I was still stricken with depression.

I didn't have my running then. Too many niggling injuries,

out of the routine. I didn't have my running friends. I was snooker, snooker, snooker. That's all I was. And all the people around me wanted snooker, and me winning, and the champagne and spliffs afterwards. They were hungry for it all the time. They were toxic.

I was on pills for anxiety and even then I couldn't get out of bed. It felt like I was wearing concrete boots. The night I won the UK Championships I went to the bar, drank two bottles of champagne, went up to my room, had a spliff and then kept drinking, all because I wasn't happy.

I woke up the next morning and did the bathroom mirror thing. Tired eyes. Lines on my forehead. A hollowness about it all.

This ain't where I want to be with it. This ain't working.

This is the place I've come to now, thirty years on from turning pro. I would still love to win every tournament I play, but I accept it's unlikely to happen. So rather than letting my happiness be defined only by winning snooker matches, I try to take pleasure from all of my day.

I think about how lucky I am to play a sport I love. I relish running with the friends I'll only see once a year at the tournament in their local town. If I get beaten early on, I'll do my punditry for Eurosport, I'll enjoy my time in the studio with Jimmy White, and I'll still finish that tournament with a smiley face in my iPhone notes.

Running in the morning, coffee at lunchtime, scone with jam in the afternoon. I know the moment will come when I'll have to get my shirt and suit on and play. But it'll be half an hour before my match, not face down in it all from the moment I wake up. The only time I need to switch into snooker mode.

I've had times at the Welsh Open in Newport where I've played an afternoon session, had an evening session coming up and walked out of the venue and gone to the cinema. A wave on my way out – see you later, don't worry, I'll be back in a bit.

The film would finish, and I'd have twenty minutes to get back for the deciding session of the final. Ten minutes before it began I'd be putting my suit on, fastening my bow tie.

It gave me no time to think about the evening shift, no time for the dark thoughts to blow in and take hold. Cue out of its case, walk straight out to the table.

I relished the reaction I'd get when I walked back in.

'Where have you been? You've got a match in a minute . . .'

I remember Steve Davis admitting later in his career that he practised far too much, purely out of guilt. It didn't make sense to me until about ten years ago, when I realised I was doing exactly the same thing – practising and practising, thinking it was the only way to get my game right.

I thought back to the days with Simon Thomas and the boys at Ilford. I'd walk in, fourteen years old, get my cue out and start playing. First frame I'd knock in a 134, missing the final pink for the 147.

I thought back to my early days on tour, all innocence, all fun. I'd arrive a few days before, like everyone else, and there would be 128 players all trying to get on six or seven practice tables. It was pointless even trying to get a slot. They were booked solid for two days. So I wouldn't bother practising. I'd go into my first match cold, and the first frame I'd win with a 120 break, and the next I'd win with a 115.

Most players in a final will think, right, I've played an afternoon session, this is a big day for me, I'd better do another twenty minutes on the practice table in between. And that way lies madness. Now, when I'm practising at tournaments, I pop a timer on my phone as I line up the first shot. As soon as the alarm goes off, that's me done for the day. Doesn't matter if

I've finished on a good shot or a bad shot, it's time to put the cue down.

It's a bit like Usain Bolt before the Olympic 100 metres final in Beijing. He didn't do a load of starting drills the night before. He went to the athletes' village and ate chicken nuggets. And Usain always got it right.

It's still strange for me, this new way. When I play badly, a part of me wonders if it was because I'd been mowing the garden, tidying the house, cleaning the patio or taking the dog for a walk. Five or ten years ago I'd never have done any of it. I was on terror alert for any distraction. Had Laila asked me then to take Osho for a walk I would have asked her if she was joking. Nothing could get in the way of practice. Now I'll have a go at her if she takes Osho, because I want to do it. It's my favourite part of the day.

Snooker can absolutely make me happy. It's just not the only thing anymore. You don't want any one thing in your life to rule you.

Remember: emotions are fickle. How you're feeling in one moment is no guarantee of how you will be feeling when you wake up tomorrow, and it's certainly not a guarantee of the truth of it all. Remember the helicopter trick. Zoom out and put all you are going through in perspective. See the whole picture, not just you, face down in it all. The bad days will probably still happen to you, as they happen to me too. So will the good. That's okay, as long as we remind ourselves it's all natural. As long as I can play and be happy again, just as I could at Ilford snooker club with Simon Thomas and the rest of the happy gang. If I can sit there watching and feel just as good, in the bright rectangles of light and the dark shadows.

Playing, swearing, winning, playing again. All of it like a dream.

13

WORLDS PART II
RULE NUMBER ONE

It's a grey evening in Sheffield, rain starting to blow in from the Peak District. A night to be indoors.

I'm walking back from the Crucible to my hotel, two sessions into the final of the 2022 World Championships. I'm 12-5 up against Judd Trump, and I'm playing well, but I'm knackered from the stress and effort and still shattered from an epic semi-final against John Higgins, and there's still the second day of this final to come. Still six more frames to win before I can think about lifting that lovely old trophy for a seventh time.

Through the lobby, into the lift. Thinking about peace and quiet after the hustle and bustle of backstage at the venue. Cue case in my hand, suit bag over my shoulder, looking forward to getting back to my room and sticking the telly on and flopping back on the sofa in the lounge. An hour or two of telly, a spot of tea, and into the bedroom for a proper kip. Lovely.

Walking up to my hotel room door. It's open.

I give it a push. There's people, everywhere – talking, laughing, drinking. Must be fifteen, twenty of them in here.

I know them all, some better than others. I like them. They're here because I invited them, at some point. I just don't want them here now. Why would I? I'm here to work, not to mess about. I wouldn't come into your office when you were trying to close a business deal and plant myself in a seat across the desk and start chatting away to you.

Leave me alone.

That's what I want to shout.

It's not the first time I've let people into my life, given them an inch and then all of a sudden they're on my doorstep, kitbag in hand, wanting to stay for four or five days, and you can't get rid of them. One year I dropped out of the Masters just so I didn't have to deal with all the stuff around it. All the people texting me for tickets. Telling me I could do it, trying to pump me up to get me across the line. Me doing my classic people-pleaser routine, and deciding not to enter one of the biggest tournaments of the season as a result.

Other times I used to deliberately lose, just to piss them off. Before I met Steve Peters, pure self-sabotage. That's how strongly I have felt about it.

'See? You were wrong. You fucked up . . .'

You get angry fast in these sort of situations. I hate being told I can do it – that I can win. I know I can do it. I don't need anyone to tell me I can. I feel like saying to them: If it's so easy, you have the cue. You have the waistcoat and the suit and the pressure.

I've said it a few times. Finally come out with it.

'How about you go and do it?'

They're never sure how to react.

A laugh, like they think I'm joking. A look at my face, the laughter uncertain now.

'Hah hah, no, you're alright, Ronnie . . .'

I know they mean well. And I know, deep down, it's my fault in the first place. Me being a people-pleaser again, finding it hard to say no, struggling with confrontation. I should be making it clear: I appreciate your support, but this is a World final. The job is hard enough as it is.

Still creating my own problems, another big life lesson for me. You think you've cracked it, and you haven't.

So I went into my bedroom and called in Robbie, my mate, the person who always stays with me in Sheffield. I told him how I felt.

'Robbie, I'm in a good place, I just need some space. Please tell everyone they've got to go.'

And Robbie went out, and told each of them politely, one by one, and gradually they all said their goodbyes and filed out, and finally – on the biggest night of my year, when anyone normal would be asleep, when I needed my rest more than any other evening – I could kick my shoes off, and make that cup of tea, and stop thinking about Judd Trump and how it would feel to win seven world titles.

Maybe that helps explain why I found the World Championships in the Covid time so much easier. The 2020 tournament was delayed to late July and early August, but that was okay with me. For almost all of it, no spectators were allowed in. The media stuff was done remotely or curtailed. The Crucible was a place of quiet and calm.

I loved it. I could go out, relax, enjoy Sheffield and be left alone. I could play, go back to my hotel, and barely see another soul. Just me and my snooker – no hype, no pressure, no friends on my sofa. I didn't need fans in the venue to get me up for it. It's the Worlds. I've been going for thirty years. I get it.

I arrived in average form. I never found my best game, not consistently. In the early rounds, in the three-session matches,

I'd have one great session and two poor ones. The good one was enough to squeak me through. As I progressed into the four-session matches I'd have one good, one half-decent and two I didn't like.

13-10 against Ding Junhui in the last sixteen. 13-10 again to get past Mark Williams in the quarter-finals. The epic 17-16 battle with Mark Selby in the semis.

I still didn't find my game in the final. Against Kyren Wilson I played half-decent in the first session to lead 6-2, a nice run in the late afternoon of three frames in a row. The second session I was horrendous, losing four frames on the spin, profiting from Kyren missing a straightforward red in the final frame to finish the first day 10-7 up.

I was there because I was just about holding it together. Blagging it, to me.

Others were telling me it was good mental skills, and maybe they're right, but it was a precarious old thing. Playing badly but not letting it show. Keeping my body language positive. Get on with the next shot, refocus, go again.

I still fell apart. You just didn't see it, watching on the telly. The falling apart would happen in my room before and after each session.

Those are the hardest times, waiting to play again. That's when the doubts swirl around. They wait until you're on your own and you're vulnerable and then they come diving in.

When you're playing well you look forward to the next session. You know you're on a roll. It's your time. You want to cash it, to play even better. When your game is in good shape you feel like you can take it anywhere. You can defend better, you can attack better.

Okay, how can we turn the screw here?

When you're struggling, you think about what's going

wrong. You've lost that ability to move through the gears, at least in your head in that moment.

Can I put this right? Why haven't I been able to put it right before? If I can't, can I fake it so my opponent still thinks I'm the man he fears, not a player sagging on the ropes?

You can't analyse your game when you're out there on the table in a World final. Out there you can't question yourself. Don't try to figure anything out. Just one ball at a time, one ball at a time . . . So this was me in that final. Playing it like Tiger Woods played the Open at Hoylake in 2006, never ripping it down the fairway but taking an iron off the tee, keeping it safe, making sure to stay out of the bunkers. I played the percentages, played conservatively rather than with abandon. I used everything I could to get the best out of myself. To give myself the best chance.

On the Monday morning I knew I had to find something, or else I would be taking Sunday's bad form on to this second day. I went on the practice table and changed my grip – made it more neutral, more balanced, so I was more compact in my stance and hitting the ball better. It was all about getting the cue ball from A to B. That was what I needed.

The third session I found my groove. Lost the first frame, but then started picking them off, with nice little unflashy breaks – a 53, a 61, a 57. 13-8 up. A 60, a 71, a 72.

I won seven frames on the bounce, by the end of that session. A gap where I could go back to my room and panic no more. Where there was nothing else to figure out. A final session that lasted only eleven minutes, because that was all I needed for a break of 96 and the last frame required.

They all feel different, the World Championships you win. The first was getting the monkey off my back. The second and the third didn't feel like they changed much. Won on instinct, not science. Quite a few players have won two, enough have won three.

The fourth in 2012? That was the best I ever played, the first full flush of the Steve Peters effect, snooker I would happily go back to at any time. 2013 was a combination of some solid play, but also using my mind.

This one, in 2020, was all mind. No strong play at all. And that brought its own particular satisfaction, its own special reward. Getting the job done, plotting my way through.

We celebrated well afterwards. Maybe my best ever night after winning a world title, because there weren't many others there with me. Not many there in my world is still about thirty people, but you have to bear in mind that in a non-Covid world there would have been about five hundred of them, the whole circus, everyone wanting a selfie with you, a phone call to their pissed mates back home.

This was just a small gathering, back at the hotel. The first attempt at mingling after the initial burst of the pandemic. The special people are the ones you try to spend time with: Laila, who had watched the final two sessions; my mates Robbie and John. My dad, done with his pacing on the pavement outside the Crucible.

There's always a last man standing at these affairs. It's never me. I stayed until about three or four in the morning, and then I just quietly sneaked off. You can't say goodbye to everyone. They won't let you leave. Just one or two who I'll whisper quietly to – look, I'm going to be gone soon. I'll tell them and then wait for my chance, and then slide away to my room. Most of the others don't even notice you've gone, anyway. They're having a good time, they're six or seven drinks in. They don't notice the undercurrents and the subplots.

Me, up in my room. Tired now, ready for a fortnight of doing not very much at all. Of leaving my cue alone. Of putting the worries and pressure and dreams away for another summer.

And so we come to my forty-seventh year. My thirtieth visit to the Crucible, a different man to the seventeen-year-old kid who arrived in 1993 and lasted that solitary first-round match against Alan McManus. Subtle flashes of grey in my sideburns, the old boy now amongst the youngsters.

The older boy, maybe. No one had won a world title at my age. That was the big stat. But I felt . . . content. In my safe space.

I didn't worry when I was 3-0 down in my first-round match against Dave Gilbert. That happens, sometimes, when you're starting out again in Sheffield. A little rust to shake off the old steel. I eased through 10-5, and I felt good again in beating Mark Allen 13-4 in the round of 16, and Stephen Maguire 13-5 in the quarter-finals. Fine-tuning as I went along, feeling the rhythm of that first ten days, the gentle acceleration. A tournament for the veterans, if you want to think of us Class of '92 that way: me, Mark Williams, John Higgins, all turning professional in 1992–3, all becoming world champions, winning the Masters and the UK Championship, all back in the semi-finals at the Crucible all these years later.

Higgins. I didn't want him at this stage, not at this point in our rivalry. Three of the last four times we'd played each other, he had come out on top: 6-1, in the semi-final of the Scottish Open; 6-5, at the English Open; 10-3, in the final of the Players Championship.

It's never good if someone has bashed you up a few times on the bounce. I hadn't been playing as I should at the Players, and he had been, and I went for my shots and he just picked me off. He played great but I didn't dig in. I wasn't prepared to die.

This time I knew I would have to be. Higgins likes playing me. He keeps beating me. Nine times we had met in semi-finals before this, and he had won seven of them. He was confident, and he wasn't going to crumble.

Ronnie, you will have to play at your absolute best here. Your game good, your head good.

And it was so tight.

4-4.

5-5.

The two of us knowing, after all these years.

Blimey, I'm in a match here.

Sticking with him. 6-6.

I was okay with that. I wanted him to sit there when I was at the table thinking, oh no, this little sod is going to keep coming at me. I'm going to have to come out and play snooker.

7-6, 8-6, 9-6.

I couldn't take the brakes off; I wanted to, but I had to make it absolutely clear to him that I was there to win.

Into the sixteenth frame, the last before the end of the final session on day one. There is a massive difference between going back to the hotel 10-6 up or 9-7.

I knew it. He knew it.

That was when I went into the pack off a regulation blue to the left middle, and a red on the edge planted into the right corner pocket.

You give a chance like that to a player like Higgins, and he cashes those chips in. He was 51 points ahead with a maximum of 51 left on the table when he lined up a straightforward black to the right corner.

And missed it.

World Championships semi-final, the Crucible, April 2022

Look at his face!

Higgins can't believe it. His head's still down.

Right. Three reds left, and I'll need to get on the black off every one, then clear up the colours. That'll bring it level. Then it's a re-spotted black.

Let's have a look at this. The black's not in an ideal position, off its spot, but I need it off this red.

Hmm. Not left myself a great angle. It might just go to the left corner, but it's a blind pocket shot – I can't see the opening from here.

The cue ball is near enough to it. I reckon I can flick this in.

Lovely. In it goes. White travelling towards the two reds on the bottom cushion, rolling up to nudge them and get on one.

Fuck. Bad cannon.

Neither red's on.

Bang my fist on the butt of my cue in anger.

There was me thinking I was gonna nick this frame. There's me thinking what this would do to him. He'd be devastated.

Okay. Safety. Usual rules here – the secret is to get the white up the other end of the table, deep into the cushions, between the imaginary tramlines running down from the yellow and green. Outside them and you've got no soldiers. The soldiers are your defence. They're what keeps your rival from the reds.

Trouble is, the black and pink have gone safe. I'm 43 behind, I need two reds and two blacks.

I could be fucked here.

Now he's under no pressure. He can leave the white down this end, like that.

I've got a chance with a red to the right middle but there's no point, because I can't get on to the black off it.

Ronnie, let's think about this. You ain't going to get many opportunities against Higgins. First chance you get in this frame, you've got to play the miracle shot. There's no point waiting for the perfect opportunity because it won't come, not against this bloke.

Safety, safety, safety.

Higgins can keep going here all day long. He's thinking, that pink and black sitting together like that are my saviour.

I'll take the white back up behind the soldiers. I'm not playing to cover him with the red. I'm just going to get the white in that area, that's all I need to focus on. Like Ray Reardon taught me. Don't worry about where the balls go, get behind the soldiers and you're fine.

Here comes the chance. White and red close to the bottom cushion, roughly on the black and pink spots. I'll still have to pot this red, pot the black, get the red, get the black.

It's a nightmare. It's the realm of the snooker gods.

It's still my chance. Red to top left, will have to travel a mile. Then I'll have to bring the white towards the black and pink on left-hand side . . .

Made it!

Crowd's going nuts . . .

I've drifted in now, arced the white to get it deeper into the cushion and round to the black. The black goes to the bottom right, but I am close to it.

It's a horrible shot.

Taking the black on, knowing the angle should take my white up towards the final red by the green spot.

Black on its way.

Left jaw, right jaw, left jaw . . . and drops.

Look at Higgins.

Now he's thinking, fuck I could lose this.

I'd like to play this last red left-handed, but I can't get settled over it, and now this is another horrible shot – using the rest, so I can't judge the pace as well. Extension on the cue so the cue don't feel like mine and I can't really feel the white when I hit it.

In. White ball travelling back down the table.

Too straight on the black. I needed more of an angle.

Pot it. Coming off the side cushion to open up a long pot at the yellow . . . and clipping the pink.

This yellow might be the hardest shot I've had to hit the whole World Championships. It's off straight. I'll have to play it with a bit of side, I'll have to get the right line to get on the green. There's no point potting this but not getting on the green. I'm playing for position.

Yes! Lovely timing on that, into the right part of the pocket, nice bit of side on the white, come round two cushions for the green.

Whoa. Now I can feel the pressure in here.

I've got to clear these up. This is a huge frame.

Quick glance at Higgins' face. It's just changed completely. Smiles in the crowd, whoops as the green goes and I come up close to the blue, but his face has collapsed. He's wondering what the fuck has gone on here.

You've gone, mate . . .

Not a great shot on the blue, not the ideal angle on the pink. Now I've hit that one a bit heavy, and I'm too close to the side cushion for my liking on this black.

Pot this and it's 53-53 and a re-spot.

It's missable.

Stop stressing about not being nearer the black. Think ball in hole.

Nailed it.

It's proper hurt him, that. It's killed him.

Got to control my emotions here. No point in making that clearance then not winning the frame.

Higgins to go first. Classic side-to-side shot, white close to the left cushion, black on the right. I'll go for the double into the left middle, but it's more about where I leave the white – yep, missed that by a mile, but the white's up tight on the cushion – awkward cueing from there.

He has to go for this. Long black on the angle to the top right corner pocket. I reckon he'll pot it.

Misses it right!

The white's travelling back. I'm on. I've got a shot to win it here.

So. Do I go left corner or middle? Too much distance going end bag. I could flick this in.

This feels like a penalty shoot-out. This has to go in.

Over it. Silence.

Thunk.

In.

10-6.

Fist-bump with Higgins. He looks . . . broken.

Out the arena. Back to my dressing room. Thinking: I'm in a war here. It's going to be tough, but I'm here to win it.

I'm going to win it.

I've never seen John Higgins quit, and I never expect to. But when I shook his hand at the end of the third session, 15-9 up, I knew he was done. The look he gave me suggested that the fight had gone out of him.

I'm not even certain he knew he was giving me that look. But it meant I went out for the final session feeling free of any pressure. Once you've broken a rival, they almost never come back.

Some of those early frames, I stole. Coming out on top in some of the early safety battles was critical; as soon as Higgins senses that you're vulnerable, that you're not playing with confidence, he's all over you. So I had to keep piling into him, and that sixteenth frame was the critical one. Higgins and Selby don't crack, not normally. To make it happen you have to be relentless. You have to make them think you're never going to crack.

It's why that win, in that semi-final, is one of the top few victories of my entire career. I might have won that way in my younger days, but only off pure instinct. This was thought-based. It was working out the cause and effect. It was something you can only do at your thirtieth World Championships, not your first.

This is the Worlds. We're here to win. Get your winning head on. Give it the full bollocks.

It would be Judd Trump in the final, after he got past Mark Williams. My preparation, the Sunday morning it began, was to pop over the road to Marks & Spencer's and have a cup of tea in the little café there.

I didn't want to be cooped up in my room. I didn't want to be downstairs in the hotel, getting badgered by people, and I didn't want to be walking the streets, bumping into everyone on their way to the Crucible. At 11 a.m. on a Sunday the café in Marks is lovely and quiet. They make a nice cup of tea. I could pick up my scone and clotted cream for later on and then stroll into the main store for some fresh socks and underwear.

Ronnie O'Sullivan, rock 'n' roll rebel.

It was a moment of joy for me. Maybe that sounds daft, but you need to be me, living in that unique moment. After that it was round the corner to Up & Running on Church Street. I love it in there – your classic running shop, a nice browse of the trainers and waterproof jackets. I'd been buying elastic laces there all week, the ones triathletes use with the little plastic lock on them. It wasn't so much the laces that worked for me, although I loved them; it was the act of going into a running shop, being around people that I liked being around, spending time in an environment I found positive and relaxing.

And it all worked for me.

Losing the first frame but winning the second with a break of 120. Going into a 3-1 lead with a cocked-hat double off three cushions on a re-spotted black, because I was playing happy and enjoying the whole weekend and attacking when the chance came. Another century in the sixth frame, a small barney with referee Oliver Martell towards the end of the session over a call he made off a Trump safety, but me not letting it stay in my head.

Into the second session, keeping calm, keeping smiling. Judd struggling a little, missing a few pots, and me moving in and keeping all the sweet momentum up. 12-5 up at the end of the Sunday, and that's not normal for a World final – not unless you're Steve Davis, or Stephen Hendry.

There are only two occasions in my Crucible career when I've frozen. When both my mind and body have felt blocked, and there's nothing I can do about it. The first was when I played John Higgins in the last session of the 2001 final. At one stage I was all over the shop. Fucking hell, I don't know how the hell I'm going to get through this game.

The other time was the Monday afternoon against Trump. The day after going back to my room and finding all those people in there having the time of their lives.

I fell apart, it was horrible, and I was lucky to squeeze two frames in the session. I could easily have lost all eight. I couldn't shift it. I couldn't seem to play my way out of it.

14-11 going into the final session. The magic, and the confidence, beginning to return. Building my breaks – an 82, an 88, a 75. 17-12 ahead, one more frame needed. A century from

Judd for 17-13, but then me back in the balls again after a nice red along the bottom cushion and a gentle cannon off another red protecting the black.

Not thinking about the finish line, like twenty-one years before against Higgins, just seeing balls and potting balls. Tidying the table.

Shouts from the crowd after the red that took me to 61 points, Trump needing snookers. More of them, louder, after the black that sealed it.

Another red, another black. Hearing the crowd loud in my ears, in that cramped space.

'Come on, Ronnie!'

It was exhaustion I felt, at the end. Taking a couple of strides over to where Judd was sitting and putting my arms around him. A proper big tight hug, holding him close, letting all the emotions come spilling out.

I can't do this no more, mate. I'm done. Count me out. You're going to have to find someone else to play with.

That's what I said to him, in that moment. That's why he looked surprised. I was just so relieved it was all over. Seventeen days that had taken so much out of me. All the pressure, all the expectation. Thirty years of trying. Too much for an old boy. An older boy.

He's a good lad, Judd. He told me I deserved to win. He said, you worked hard. It's yours.

I wasn't thinking about the numbers. Not yet thinking that I'd equalled the seven world titles of Hendry. I never chased the numbers. Not bothered, in the moment, I'd just become the oldest world champion in history, a year past one of my old coaches, Ray Reardon.

I wanted to hug the kids. Lily and Ronnie, and my dad. I said the same to them: I love you, and I can't do this no more.

I know I have, today, but I just can't. If I keep trying to do this, there's not going to be a happy ending. And we've got so close to a happy ending.

The synchronicity of them in the photo, ten years on. Thinking how hard it had been, sometimes. The relationship with their mother. Looking at Lily and reflecting: I never thought I would be here with you now, me being fit and healthy, you grown up into a lovely girl, and you're happy and I'm happy. Seldom a smooth ride for any of us, but least we're here to talk about it and support each other.

Because I never thought I would ever be there, in that moment. Holding the trophy for a seventh time, with my family around me. I thought I would be beaten, destroyed – a weak man, bludgeoned into a corner or long gone. So many troubles, and financial pressures, and stress, just to keep everything going, to try to play the sport.

Instead, seeing the kids leading their own lives, with their own friends. Being overwhelmed with gladness that I had been able to keep my end of the bargain and be healthy at the end of it. Standing there with my dad, as the silver and red and blue ticker tape fell from the ceiling. Remembering the feeling when he went away and I was a lost kid. All those impossible, lonely times, and now a night I never thought would happen.

I am not a victim. I never have been. But I am proud of myself – proud I have been able to not fall apart, to get everything done and hold it all together, to make the people I care about proud. And more of those emotions came tumbling out when I walked into the Eurosport studio and saw Jimmy White. It hit me all over again.

I wasn't surprised to feel so utterly shattered. The Worlds get harder and harder. It's always a massive drain, now. I wasn't surprised Jimmy looked so overjoyed. I'm more detached from snooker now. I've managed to navigate myself to the point where I can enjoy the game whether I win or lose. I don't get the same highs I did as a kid, but I don't get the same lows that come with them.

Jimmy is on his own path. He still loves the idea of winning. He'll talk about me winning ten world titles and ten UK Championships, and that's fine. I feel Jimmy's love and I feel his support. It's fantastic he's so passionate about these achievements. It's just I'm not, in the same way. I decided I don't want to be defined by snooker.

Anyway, I think the snooker gods are doing it for Jimmy as well. They're not just doing it for me. The snooker gods think, alright, even if you don't want this, Ron, we're sure it'll make people who love snooker happy.

It took me a while to process it all. I'd never felt quite the same as this in winning any of the other six. I couldn't believe what had happened. I went from freezing in the afternoon – how the fuck am I going to play tonight? – to coming out in the evening ready to hit Trump with some bombs. Knowing I had to do what Hendry taught me: play the shot the right way, play a game that sends the message I wasn't frozen anymore.

So we stayed up late, that night. The kids, my dad. A return to the pre-Covid days, about five hundred people knocking around. My lot, their lot, all the snooker lot. Too many for me, the whole hectic madness of it doing my head in. I wanted to go to bed and chill out. Have a beer in my room, lob my suit in the corner. I had a smoke, but that made me almost pass out, and I was sitting there at one point unable to speak and everyone around me panicking and wanting to call an ambulance.

I was fine. I just needed my bed. I told them I was okay, and legged it to my room. And the next morning was like I was walking on air. I slept beautifully, as if I'd completed an Ironman triathlon. The Crucible is never a sprint distance, and it takes its toll.

Ray Reardon used to say to me, 'There's only one tournament, the World Championships. All the others, they're just practice.' He should know. He won six of them.

The good feeling lasts, if you let it. You, the world champion. The world number one. When the first shot is played of the new season, everyone says, okay, we go again. But that World Championship tag stays with you all through that season, no matter what else may come to pass. It stays with you for years to come.

And you have to enjoy it all, or it means nothing. Rule number one, of all my rules, is to be grateful you're enjoying playing the game. Rule number two: don't forget rule number one.

Victory at the Worlds means different things to different people. If you ask John Parrott and Dennis Taylor and Ken Doherty are they happy to have won one, they'll tell you they're still over the moon. There was a time I was happy with one, because I feared it might never happen. Then once you win one, you want to win two. You get to three, and it isn't much different.

When I won it four times, it was a game-changer. I was content. I thought, if I never win another one, I've done okay. Four puts me in the top five or six players of all time – not as good as Steve Davis and Ray Reardon and Stephen Hendry, but they were different animals. I was only about talent at that stage. I didn't feel as driven as them; I didn't have their mental strength, so I had to make up for that through shot-making and artistry.

Then I realised I needed more. I needed the mind, too.

Artistry won me games, but it can fall apart. I loved watching Alex Higgins and Jimmy. It was beautiful. But over seventeen days in Sheffield, did you put your money on those two, or on Davis and Hendry?

That's why the sixth title in 2020 meant so much to me. I'd put together all my life lessons and I'd used them all. I'd become as strong mentally as my heroes. I could win with both artistry and the mind. I was at the dinner table with Davis and Reardon, guys who have become the masters of their sport, like Arnold Palmer and Tom Watson and Gary Player.

To get to seven? That was the pinch-me moment. Now it's Tiger Woods and Jack Nicklaus. And what gives it meaning is that I could finally appreciate it all. Enjoying it, and so grateful to be doing so.

EPILOGUE

There's a clip you can find, if you want to, of the first television interview I ever did. I'm eleven years old, in a white shirt with matching white bow tie and a cream-coloured waistcoat. Rosy cheeks, happy smile, glass of lemonade on the table in front of me.

It's Danny Baker chatting to me. He asks me about Steve Davis, he asks me if I'm going to the top. Then he says to me: 'How big do you want to be?'

This is an easy question. I've thought about it a lot. So I nod, and I tell him.

'About five foot ten?'

Your dreams change, as you get older. One day it's all about how tall you're going to be. Then it was about playing the perfect game of snooker. For a long period in my life, that was all that mattered to me.

Now it has moved on again. It's early April, and I'm getting ready for my thirty-first World Championships. Practising, plotting, trying not to obsess.

I don't ever want to get carried away by winning the Worlds. I don't want to get sucked in again. As soon as you get me on that relentless search for perfection and it becomes all about the winning, I'll become an unhappier person. The sport will take me back into the dark places.

There's only so much you can take, so many times you can keep getting yourself up for it. I'm at the point now where I want to look after my sanity, my health, my mind. Do I want to have a great last thirty years of my life, or do I want to have an awful last thirty years because I lost the plot again?

I think I've taken more control of my life now. More control of my dreams. I don't need another world title. I don't need another tournament. I want to look after my family, to work but to enjoy my life too. To run, and to cook, and to have time for the people that matter. To be a better person for them.

I don't think about an eighth world title. Maybe I'll have one by the time you read this. If my game is in good shape and the signs are right, I am prepared to dig deep.

But I will not capitulate. I will not obsess. I will stay in love with snooker by setting myself free from it.

I hope some of the things I've shared will help you in your own career and your own life. The lessons I've learned about addiction and self-sabotage, about perspective and the pursuit of perfection. About understanding your unique physical and emotional thresholds, about how fickle those emotions can be. The trick shots and strategies: setting boundaries; making connections to good people; playing with your own personal dimmer switch.

I wonder, sometimes, what the Ronnie of twenty years ago, the Ronnie in rehab, what he'd think if he could see me now. The kid gone all paranoid, lost in substance abuse. A person he didn't want to be, a person who had to find himself again.

I think he'd be shocked. By the running, by how sensible I've become. Me, giving other people ideas on how they could live their lives? The staying in, the friends who aren't flash. All those world titles, for sure. I think he'd be happy, with what was coming next.

I wonder what the Ronnie of ten years ago would think. The one who took a year out from snooker and didn't realise he would come back to it. Who didn't understand yet that he needed a purpose in his life. Who saw that his phone stopped ringing, when he was no longing playing and earning, and so worked out who his real friends were.

I think he'd be happy, too. At the balance he would go on to find. Not all snooker or no snooker, but enough snooker to get up each day, and enough pleasure and satisfaction elsewhere in his life to be able to win and lose and treat it both the same. To miss a shot and walk away smiling.

The next ten years? I've thought about taking my athletics coaching badges. The best nights of my life were down at the track in Woodford Green on a Tuesday and Thursday evening. The times I took my daughter running and gave her a little advice, the times I've shared snooker knowledge with young players on the up – these have been the most rewarding.

I might play snooker for another two years. Maybe I'll push it out to three, or four. When I pick up my cue again at the start of a new season it's like a workman going back to his tools. It's a commitment to work, to the long hours. A commitment to the enjoyment it can bring.

Coming back to snooker has always taken me to a good place. The silence when you're alone on a practice table, just you and the balls and your mind. A competitor, in his safe space, in control.

Here are all the things I'm not. The things they say about me, the things you might have thought were true. Ronnie's a rebel. Ronnie's just talent. Ronnie hates snooker. Ronnie can't be arsed.

Now you know.

You're either a fighter or you're not a fighter. It's something you're given. And I know I have that in me. Resilience, courage, determination.

When the anger and frustration want to take over now, I'm better at handling it. I don't let it get the better of me. I'll have the bad day, but the next morning I'm back at it.

No one can take this game away from me. It's all there, if I want it.

Thirty-one years at the Crucible, forty-seven years old and still going. A lifetime of triumphs, and mistakes, and learning.

Unbreakable, after it all.

IMAGE CREDITS

Page one
Right © Mirrorpix via Getty Images
Left © Bob Thomas via Getty Images
Above © New Licensing/*Sun*

Page two
Top left © Robert Hallam/Shutterstock
Bottom left © Coloursport
Top right © News UK Ltd/Shutterstock
Bottom right © PA Images/Alamy

Page three
Top left © PA Images/Alamy
Bottom left © Tom Shaw via Getty Images
Top right © PA Images/Alamy
Bottom right © Graham Hughes/Mirrorpix

Page four
Top left © Shutterstock
Bottom left © Ronnie O'Sullivan
Top right © Ronnie O'Sullivan
Bottom right © Backgrid

Page five
Top left © Gareth Copley via Getty Images
Bottom left © Zuma Press, Inc./Alamy
Right © Zuma Press, Inc./Alamy

Page six
Top © Action Plus Sports Images/Alamy
Bottom left © Ronnie O'Sullivan
Bottom right © Jason Francis

Page seven
Top left © Ronnie O'Sullivan
Top right © Hassan Hajjaj
Bottom © Alamy

Page eight
Top © Lewis Storey via Getty Images
Bottom © Lewis Storey via Getty Images